Passion Killers

A play

John Godber

Samuel French — London
New York - Toronto - Hollywood

ISBN 0 573 01868 5

Please see page iv for further copyright information

PASSION KILLERS

First performed in a co-production between Hull Truck Theatre Company and Derby Playhouse on 9th April 1994. It opened the newly refurbished Hull Truck Theatre. This revised version of the play toured extensively in 1995. The cast was as follows:

Tom	Gordon Kane
Gail	Susan Cookson
Andy	Daniel O'Brien
Lynne	Jacqueline Naylor
Barbie	Charlotte Bellamy
Ray	Julian Knight
Scott	Richard Hollick
Karen	Jacqueline Naylor
Trish	Susan Cookson

Directed by John Godber
Designed by Liam Doona
Lighting by George Morris
Music by Chris Madin

COPYRIGHT INFORMATION

(See also page ii)

Licences for amateur performances are issued subject to the understanding that it shall be made clear in all advertising matter that the audience will witness an amateur performance; that the names of the authors of the plays shall be included on all programmes; and that the integrity of the authors' work will be preserved.

The Royalty Fee is subject to contract and subject to variation at the sole discretion of Samuel French Ltd.

In Theatres or Halls seating Four Hundred or more the fee will be subject to negotiation.

In Territories Overseas the fee quoted above may not apply. A fee will be quoted on application to our local authorized agent, or if there is no such agent, on application to Samuel French Ltd, London.

VIDEO-RECORDING OF AMATEUR PRODUCTIONS

Please note that the copyright laws governing video-recording are extremely complex and that it should not be assumed that any play may be video-recorded for whatever purpose without first obtaining the permission of the appropriate agents. The fact that a play is published by Samuel French Ltd does not indicate that video rights are available or that Samuel French Ltd controls such rights.

CHARACTERS

Tom, *thirty-eight, journalist*
Gail, *thirty-five, his wife, university lecturer*
Andy, *thirty-seven, businessman*
Lynne, *thirty-four, his wife*
Barbie, *twenty-one, travel rep*
Ray, *twenty-two, holiday-maker*
Scott, *twenty-two, holiday-maker*
Karen, *thirty-five, holiday-maker*
Trish, *thirty-one, holiday-maker*

The action takes place in a dining-room in England and in various parts of an hotel in Spain

Time — the present

SYNOPSIS OF SCENES

ACT I

Scene 1	Dining-room. England. Evening
Scene 2	Hotel lobby area, Spain. Day
Scene 3	Hotel exterior. Night
Scene 4	Hotel patio area. Night
Scene 5	Hotel poolside area. Day

ACT II

Scene 1	Hotel patio area. Night
Scene 2	Hotel poolside area. Morning
Scene 3	Hotel poolside area. Day
Scene 4	Hotel poolside area. Night
Scene 5	Dining-room. England. Evening

NOTES

The Set

In the original production of **PASSION KILLERS**, the composite set representing the Spanish hotel was hidden during the first scene by dust sheets and a plethora of paint pots, which were easily struck to reveal the set behind. The dust sheets and paint pots were returned to these original positions for the last scene. The author points out that the setting for England can be fairly notional, but that for Spain should be more real.

Incidental Music

A licence issued by Samuel French Ltd to perform this play does not include permission to use the Incidental music specified in this copy. Where the place of performance is already licensed by the PERFORMING RIGHT SOCIETY a return of the music used must be made to them. If the place of performance is not so licensed then application should be made to the Performing Right Society, 29 Berners Street, London W1.

A separate and additional licence from PHONOGRAPHIC PERFORMANCES LTD, Ganton House, Ganton Street, London W1 is needed whenever commercial recordings are used.

ACT I

Scene 1

The dining-room of Tom's and Gail's house somewhere in Hull

The Lights come up

Tom and Gail are entertaining their friends, Andy and Lynne. They have just finished a large meal. They are drinking wine and coffee and are all very relaxed. They have been friends for some time and argue easily

Tom They do ——
Andy I don't believe you.
Tom They do ——
Andy They don't. They can't.
Tom Of course they can.
Andy I don't believe you.
Lynne Tom never lies, Andy, you should know that.
Tom They love each other, no matter what they said, they love each other.
Andy It's not love. You said to your mother, "Congratulations on making it to your ruby wedding anniversary," and she said, "Never again." Well, I'm sorry, but that is not love.
Lynne What did your dad say?
Tom It was a joke.
Gail He stood there shaking his head. He couldn't believe they'd actually made it.
Lynne He couldn't believe she'd said it, you mean?
Andy They're stuck in a routine.
Tom You don't understand their affections.
Lynne His parents are going for gold.
Andy Look, even they don't love any more. For their ruby wedding, my dad took my mum on the Orient Express.
Tom He can afford it.
Andy They never spoke to each other, until Zurich.
Gail Actually it was a good night. His Uncle Jack told me he loved me.
Tom He's a womanizer, it runs in the family.
Gail He's not my type. I like men with their own teeth.
Tom So I'm still in with a chance.

Gail Forty years.
Andy We're all doomed.
Gail I think there's something positive about it.
Tom Lifers only get twenty-five.
Lynne Mine lasted forty and then my dad told mum that he'd met somebody else. He just wanted a new start. After all that time?
Andy Her dad's great. Good golfer.
Lynne He is actually, he's in his second youth.
Andy I hope we don't last that long.
Lynne Why?
Andy We'll have nothing to talk about.
Gail Tom's too close to his parents.
Tom (*sarcastically*) She's funny.
Gail Tom's mother has an obsession with bedclothes.
Andy Kinky.
Tom You can see the irony a mile off. There she is talking about beds, and bedding, and why? Well, my thesis is because she recognizes that we are born in them and we die in them and her and my poor dad haven't done anything in theirs for years. Except for the odd bowel mishap. It's guilt that drives her on.
Gail We all have guilt you know, it's not just the Catholics.
Tom Why did they ever stay together?
Andy It must be for the sex.
Tom It makes you think.
Lynne It makes you think why any of us stay together.

A moment's awkwardness

Andy (*of Gail*) I think you look radiant tonight. Don't you think she does?
Gail He's awful.
Lynne I can't control him.
Andy (*to Lynne*) You look radiant as well, my darling.
Lynne He's such a creep.
Tom I feel guilty because when I sell my labour power I don't put my life at risk. I'm a journalist.
Gail And don't we know it.
Lynne He wants to get back to his roots. Don't you, Tom?
Tom No, it's too real for me.
Gail That's why he left teaching.
Tom It isn't.
Gail The working-class charmers were too much for him.
Tom Now that is funny that is. That's really funny.

Pause

Gail We're sending each other crazy at the moment.
Tom We're not.
Gail You see what I mean?
Tom We're all right, it's just that we're ready for a break. I mean, last week it was the anniversary and now Gail's tied up until July. We've got the bloody decorators in. We're at it non-stop. You know what the Buddhists say, "Let there be space between your love." Well, there's no space. But we're all right most of the time, aren't we?
Gail Most of the time.
Tom I mean, sometimes we actually find time to talk to each other.
Gail Ho, ho.
Andy Are you serious?
Gail Yeah, we're fine, Andy, honest.
Andy About having a break?
Tom What do you mean?
Lynne That's a good idea.
Andy I mean, how serious are you about having a break?
Tom Serious, why?
Lynne He's going to Spain at the weekend.
Tom I can't go without her.
Lynne Course you can, that's the whole point.
Gail I'd go without you.
Tom Would you?
Gail For a week in the sun? Tell you what, you go into the department, I'll go with Andy.
Andy It's a deal. Me and Gail, yes please!
Gail Look at his face.
Tom How long is it for?
Andy Ten days.
Lynne He goes twice a year. It means I can have my mother over. You should see us, we go through the house.
Gail What about the kids, don't they miss him?
Lynne For a few days.
Andy Oh, thank you, we're a close family as you can see.
Tom How come there's a ticket?
Andy Patrick's dropped out.
Tom How much is it?
Gail Oh God, I'll pay for him.
Andy It's a gift, for Gail.

Tom No, we can't accept that.

Andy Look, I'm going to be golfing all the time, so if you want to lounge about in the sun it's there. As I see it there's only one drawback.

Tom What's that?

Andy We have to share a room.

Tom It's off.

Lynne There might be a story in it.

Gail Hemingway's done that coast. *Death in the Afternoon.*

Lynne She's bright that one.

Tom No, I'd better not.

Lynne Why not? Give Gail a break. Hey, when they're away we could paint the town red.

Gail Where in Spain, Andy?

Andy Well, it's usually the Costa del Sol, but I couldn't get in so it's Costa Blanca. Benidorm.

Tom That's a definite no.

Gail For golf?

Andy Altea Don Cayo. It's about five miles out. Fly to Alicante, hire a car. Tee off at seven, back to the hotel – actually, I was lucky to get booked in there, I took the last room they had – back to the hotel, a few little drinkies and then bed.

Gail Oh yeah?

Andy It's all above board believe me.

Lynne Do you think I'd let him go if it wasn't?

Gail Benidorm, Tom, Spain's Blackpool, back to your roots?

Tom Very funny.

Andy Have you played much golf?

Tom How about, none.

Gail We did that crazy golf thing at Southport.

Tom Not the same though, is it?

Gail Same principle.

Lynne The two of you out there, I can just imagine it.

Tom We hardly know each other.

Andy Course we do.

Lynne You'll have a riot, non-stop arguing.

Tom I know, but sharing a room?

Gail He's shy, aren't you?

Lynne Have you got something that you don't want Andy to see, Tom?

Tom A spotty bum.

Gail He's such a charmer!

Andy Nowhere to bring the women back to, eh?

Tom That's absolutely right.

Andy So it's on then, is it?
Gail Course it is.
Tom Doesn't seem right going away without Gail.
Andy Why, doesn't she trust you?
Gail I do …
Andy Miles of sandy beaches, Tom?
Gail Oh, he's off. Alan Whicker the second.
Andy Strapping Germans and Swedes all over the Lavante Beach.
Gail It's looking good.
Andy *Dos San Miguel, por favor*.
Gail He's got him hooked.
Andy Sun and sea.
Gail He's packing.
Andy Clear cloudless skies.
Gail He's at the airport.
Andy Miles of breasts on the beaches.
Tom I hate flying.
Gail He's checking in.
Andy Cocktails by the *Rosamar* pool.
Gail It's turbulent.
Tom Pass the sick-bag.
Andy Sunburn everywhere.
Tom We're coming into land.
Andy Nubile bodies?
Gail He's there, he's there.

Tom grins. They are all enjoying the game

Lynne What about the golf?
Gail Yeah what happened to the golf?
Andy What?
Lynne The golf.
Andy Oh yeah and if we have any time we'll play some golf.

All enjoy the banter; they all laugh

Music

Black-out

Scene 2

Spain. Night

A large composite set, with different levels, alcoves and entrances, painted almost entirely white, representing the lobby area of an hotel, parts of the hotel exterior and various areas around it. There is possibly a diving-board fixed on stage, its far tip off stage, which can be used as an entrance

The Lights come up on the lobby area. The light has a very different quality from that in Scene I. *The music fades*

Barbie, the club rep, is in the lobby area. She is a young woman in her mid-twenties, very brown, and extremely attractive

Ray, a very young man, struggles on to the stage with a large case

Barbie (*shouting to Ray*) Hi, hiya … Come on, we're waiting, where've you been? You're going to miss all the fun. Get yourself up here. Gatwick?
Ray I can hardly breathe.
Barbie Can you manage?
Ray Just about.
Barbie (*helping to lift a case*) What have you got in here?
Ray I think my heart's gunna burst.
Barbie How long are you here for?
Ray A fortnight.
Barbie Are you on your own?
Ray On my own out here, no way. Are you thick?
Barbie I'm getting there.
Ray Scott's still on the bus.
Barbie What's he doing?
Ray Chatting up some women probably.
Barbie Oh right.
Ray He's a right maniac …
Barbie Are you Gatwick?
Ray No, Fullwood. Ray Fullwood.
Barbie No, did you fly from Gatwick?
Ray Oh sorry, Gatwick, yeah. I thought you said was my name Gatwick.
Barbie What's it like in England?
Ray Pea soup. Some flights are delayed.
Barbie As usual.
Ray What's the weather been like?
Barbie Sunny.

Ray Sunny.
Barbie It was ninety-two last week.
Ray Frying.
Barbie That's right.
Ray Ninety-two.
Barbie Last week.
Ray What will it be this week?
Barbie Hot.
Ray If I get any hotter I'll pass out.
Barbie You won't need all that lot.
Ray I always say I'm travelling light and ——
Barbie Yeah, I see ——
Ray Is this the right hotel?
Barbie Yeah, this is the *Rosamar*, it's an overflow for Club Holidays, most of them are over at the *Victoria*. There's just a few of you in here, so ——
Ray Best behaviour.
Barbie Well ...
Ray No jumping off the balconies, right ...
Barbie If you could avoid it.
Ray Is it going to be a busy fortnight?
Barbie Don't worry, I'll make sure of that.

Scott, a very attractive lean youth in his early twenties, enters with a colourful holdall

Scott Oh ay, oh ay, oh ay, oh ay.
Barbie Are you with the Club?
Scott With the Club or in the club?
Ray Excellent.
Barbie Either?
Scott I'm with the Club, at the moment.
Ray But it could all change.
Barbie Could it?
Ray It could with him, women love him.
Barbie I can see that ...
Scott Hallo.
Barbie Hi.
Scott Hallo hallo.
Ray Double hallo.
Scott (*to Ray*) Very hallo.
Barbie Where are you from?
Scott Look at that, straight in, not even an introduction. Never you mind ...
Ray He's brilliant.

Barbie You here for the fortnight?
Scott No, two weeks. (*He laughs*)
Barbie Great.
Ray Brilliant.
Scott Where you from?
Barbie All over.
Scott All over what? (*He laughs*)
Barbie There's a free drink at the bar, but we're running a bit late because of the delays.
Ray We had a skinful on the plane anyway.
Barbie OK if you just want to get cosy for a few minutes …
Scott Best offer I've had all day.
Ray It's the only offer I've had.
Barbie I'll explain what the plan for tonight is.

Scott and Ray make themselves cosy amongst their cases. Barbie goes through her usual routine

Barbie Because of the time I suggest we dump the bags, have a quick splash ——
Scott A quick what?
Barbie — and then get back down here. The main hotel is the *Victoria*, and all the facilities are yours to use, and obviously because you're staying here you can use all the *Rosamar* facilities as well: the pool, the bar, anything. The pool here is bigger than the pool at the *Victoria*.
Ray (*sings*) Ours is bigger than theirs.
Scott Prove it.
Ray Is this all there is?
Barbie Manchester flights have gone down already. When we go down to the old town I'll show you everything.
Scott What, everything?
Barbie Well, nearly.
Scott Double hallo.
Barbie We'll call in at *Lennon's*, *Gigolo's* and *Penelope's* which is really great. I think. Then we can have a think about various activities that you can sign up for during the week. I suggest all of you sign up for the buggy ride, and the Aqualand, they're really great. And then there's *Rancho Grande* which is an absolutely outrageous barbecue where you can eat and drink as much as you like, and go completely crazy. That's really great.
Scott Hallo.
Barbie OK.
Ray Hallo.
Barbie And if there's anything that you want me for at any time just give me a shout.

Scott Give you a what?
Barbie Shout.
Ray We're shouting already.
Barbie Oh, and I'm Barbie.
Ray You certainly are.
Barbie Any questions?
Scott Yeah, how great is *Penelope's*, Barbie?
Ray It's really great, isn't it?
Barbie Yeah, it's really great. Shall we go? Do you want any help?
Scott What do you think we are?
Barbie Now you don't want me to answer that, do you?
Ray Look out.

Scott and Ray begin to get their belongings together. Barbie collects her belongings

Trish and Karen enter. Both are in their early thirties. Karen is extremely brash, aggressive and fiesty. Trish is attractive

Trish About bleeding time …
Karen Is this it?
Trish Well, ask her.
Ray Must be a witches' convention.
Karen This the *Rosa*-whatsit … ?
Trish We got on the wrong bus.
Scott (*to Ray*) Come on, nip the bags up and grab a beer.
Ray Hallo, goodbye …

Ray and Scott exit

Karen What a cock-up, honest. We got on the bleeding "Young at Heart" bus.
Trish God knows what ——
Karen It was the "Young at Heart" bus. I looked, I could only see "Young", so we got on.
Trish Wishful thinking that was.
Karen Talk about laugh. Me and her are the only two on the bus under fifty.
Trish I thought it was quiet.
Karen I says to her, I think we're on the wrong bus.
Trish Most of 'em were dead. I thought look out, we're on the wrong bus.
Karen We couldn't pull anything on that, could we?
Trish It'd probably come off in your hand, if you did.
Karen We had a quick drink, and everyone scarpered.
Barbie Oh right, you're the two from East Midlands?

Karen We've been running around the coast for two hours.
Trish You haven't got a fag, have you?
Barbie I wondered about you — thought you'd cancelled …
Trish I'm gagging.
Karen She's smoked all mine.
Trish I hate flying. I've got to have a fag or I can't get on. They have to back me on like a donkey.
Barbie Let me just check and ... erm … (*She looks in her bag and produces a computerized chart*)
Karen Posh, innit?
Trish We got on the wrong bus...
Karen Have we got a sea view?
Trish Should have.
Karen I'm dying for a loo.
Trish I went ——
Karen I didn't.
Trish — on the bus …
Barbie Singer and Ward?
Karen Karen and Trish.
Barbie Oh right. Well, you're in the right place.
Karen For a change.
Barbie Shall we get you checked in?
Karen Yeah, we're knackered.
Barbie We're meeting down here in ten minutes and then we're going downtown.
Trish Oh right, in at the deep end.
Barbie That's what the Club's all about.
Trish We're only on it because it's cheap.
Barbie Good for you.
Trish We don't want to enter the "Miss Wet T-shirt" competition.
Karen You might not.
Trish She's in for anything, she is.
Karen What time does the bar open?
Barbie It would be easier to tell you when it's closed.
Trish When is it?
Barbie It isn't.
Trish Oh, right …
Barbie I'm joking.
Trish Hey, do you think we'll be all right?
Karen Course we will.
Barbie What do you mean?
Trish Well, do you think we'll fit in?
Barbie Why shouldn't you?

Karen Course we will, she's paranoid.
Trish Well, I haven't been on one of these before.
Karen Neither have I.
Trish We lied about our age at the travel agent. I mean I'm thirty-one. She's nearly thirty-six.
Karen Why don't you shut your big gob …
Trish Singer by name …
Barbie It's all right, I won't tell anyone.
Trish I thought they might …
Karen Check up?
Barbie Is it just the one holiday a year?
Trish Worse luck.
Karen Main one.
Barbie Well, enjoy it, you probably deserve it.
Karen More than you'd ever know, I'm telling you.

Barbie starts to get their cases together

Trish I am dying for a fag.
Barbie So what sort of work do you do?
Trish I work for the Health Authority ——
Karen In a laundry.
Trish — and she's into condoms.
Karen I work in a chemist; listen to her — you little ——
Trish Well, it's true.
Karen I sell 'em, that's all.
Barbie Well, you should feel at home here then.
Trish Where are we?
Barbie Check at reception …

Scott enters, carrying a drink

Scott Excuse me, ladies — let me through, I am a doctor.

Trish and Karen exit. As they exit, Ray enters with a drink

Scott Right, we're ready.
Barbie That was quick.
Scott Oh ay, I'm great at getting my gear off.
Barbie Right.
Scott So remember that.
Barbie Where's that accent from then?
Scott Nosy, aren't you?

Barbie I collect accents.
Scott Oh ay, well, guess: if you get it right, you win a prize.
Barbie Lancashire, isn't it?
Scott Ah you're wrong, no. It's Yorkshire, all right? You owe me for that. Ah wrong, tough. Ahhhh.
Ray Everybody thinks that. Guess where I'm from.
Barbie No, I couldn't.
Ray London.
Barbie Really?
Ray Yeah.
Scott Have you seen the pool?
Ray Yeah.
Scott It's massive.
Ray Is it man-made do you think?
Scott No, it's natural, you dick.
Ray It isn't.
Scott It's massive.
Ray I know.
Scott Hey, what about them two?
Ray What?
Scott Yeah.
Ray Naaa.
Scott Yeah.
Ray You reckon?
Scott Worth a shot, hey Barbie?
Barbie Oh yeah, I'm sure you'll be in there …
Ray Whaaa?
Scott Yeah.
Ray Well, yeah.
Scott Where we going first?
Barbie Eager, aren't you?
Scott I've waited eight months for this. We booked it about five years ago … I've been counting the days.
Ray Five years?
Scott I'm making a point, you dollop!
Barbie Why don't you get another drink then we'll go down.
Scott Are you trying to get me drunk?
Barbie Would I do that to you?
Scott Dunno. Do you want one?
Ray Hallo!
Scott (*sings*) Hallo hallo hallo …

Scott exits

Barbie sits with Ray

Barbie Room OK?
Ray Dunno, I haven't had time to look at it. We dumped our bags and came straight down. We might have put our stuff in a bog for all I know.
Barbie Have you decided what you're going to sign up for?
Ray Everything I think.
Barbie That's the spirit.
Ray Yeah, everything.
Barbie You know it's extra?
Ray Yeah, I've got the cash, haven't I?
Barbie A glutton for punishment, eh?
Ray I always sign up for everything.
Barbie Have you been out here before then?

Trish and Karen enter

Karen Bleeding hell, all go, innit?
Barbie You'll get used to it.
Karen No, I'm not complaining, that's what we're here for.
Trish Coooor hot, isn't it?
Barbie This is Ray. He's from London.
Trish Hallo, Ray.
Ray Hallo.
Barbie God knows where his mate's from. This is Trish and Karen. Karen's into condoms.
Karen I'll bleeding kill her …
Trish You here for the fortnight?
Ray No, fourteen days… (*Laughing at his own joke*) Haaaaa.
Trish We are. I'm knackered already, don't think I'll be able to take the pace. Mind you, you'll be all right, you're only young, aren't you? Look at us, we're like two grandmother greys.
Ray Yeah, I know.
Karen You speak for yourself.
Trish Stifling, isn't it?

Andy appears. He is wearing shorts and a shirt, sandals and no socks

Andy Do you mind if I — the bar's — packed.
Barbie Just arrived?
Andy About an hour. From Manchester.
Barbie You're not with the Club?
Andy No.

Barbie I thought not.
Andy You lot all on a package then?
Karen A fortnight.
Andy Lovely.
Karen Not bad.
Trish Nice hotel, from what we've seen.
Karen Yeah, don't blink here, mate, or you'll miss something …
Barbie Are you here by yourself?
Andy No … he's just …
Trish So we should get a good tan.
Karen I want to be like an 'andbag when I go back.
Andy A few holes-in-one'll suit me.
Trish Holes-in-one eh? What do they shout? Fore, innit?
Andy Four, five, six — anything.
Trish Seven …

Scott returns with another bottle of beer

Scott All right?
Andy Yeah?
Scott You with us … ?
Andy No …
Scott I was going to say … Bloody hell, I thought my dad had turned up.
Andy No problem.
Scott I thought, hallo, he's gunna need a walking frame come the end of the week. Get that down your neck. (*He gives the drink to Ray*)
Karen What are you then?
Andy Ten days.
Karen Ohphhh, ten.
Scott When are we going down to *Lennon's*, then, Barbie?
Ray Yeah, put another prawn on the barbie, Barbie.
Barbie (*acting up to Ray*) Soon, darling, soon.
Scott Got a good tan, 'aven't yer?
Barbie Well, I've been out here for years.
Scott You speak Spanish then?
Barbie Yes, do you?
Scott Naaa.
Ray Oggy.
Scott Oi.
Ray Oggy.
Scott Oi.
Ray Oggy Oggy Oggy.
All Oi Oi Oi.

Tom enters. He looks rather less trendy than Andy. He wears sandals and socks

Tom Where've you been?
Andy Just … er …
Tom I still can't get through, I'll have to phone later. Are we going to get a … ermm?
Andy This is Tom.
All Hallo, Tom.
Scott (*shouting*) Hallo, Tom.
Tom Hallo, everybody. Food?
Scott (*slightly sinister*) Hallo, Tom.
Tom Good job I didn't bring a cat.
Trish Why's that?
Tom Well, I couldn't swing it in the bedroom, that's for sure.
Trish Would it be a tom? (*She laughs*)
Tom The beds are based on a design from Dachau.
Trish You what?
Andy A fortnight …
Tom Whoooooo.
Andy Bloody hell …
Scott Tom? Tom?
Tom What?
Scott Are you a drum?
Tom No, funnily enough.
Scott What are you then?

Ray moves to stand in front of Tom

Ray Oggy.

Silence

Tom What?
Ray Oggy!
Tom (*trying*) Oggy!
Ray What?
Tom Eh?
Trish Just say Oi.
Tom Oi what?
Ray Oggy Oggy Oggy.
Tom Oggy Oggy Oggy.
Barbie You're not going to get it, are you?

Tom I think it's too complicated for me.
Scott (*a type of football chant*) Oh ay, oh ay, oh ay, oh ay.
Trish Oh ay, look out, we're off. This is what they want.
Karen Is he bleeding crackers?
Tom Are we going to make a move?
Andy Can do. (*He begins to move away*) Nice to.
Scott Oh ay, oh ay, oh ay …
Barbie Are you coming down to Lennon's?
Tom Is it John's or Yoko's?
Barbie Both …
Scott (*chanting*) In the pool, in the pool, in the pool, in the pool.
Ray In the pool.
Barbie Oh no.
Scott In the pool, in the pool, in the pool …
Barbie Oh no, no …
Scott Yeah. Tom, grab her, you twat …
Ray In the pool, in the pool …

The rest laugh hopelessly. Ray picks up the chant, and begins to join in. Scott and Ray grab Barbie. She knows what they are after. They throw her into the pool, which is off stage

Barbie disappears off into the pool

Ray and Scott make an enormous cheer and follow her off

Tom Are we going to get off or what?
Trish This is brilliant.
Andy That's right.
Tom Hilarious.
Trish I'm not going in, no way, I'm not going in, Tom, you'll have to save me!
Tom Right.
Karen It's a laugh, innit?
Trish He's bloody funny, that little Ray — isn't he cute?
Karen They're gunna be a laugh, they are.
Tom Anyway …
Andy Yeah yeah …
Karen Where are you from then?
Tom York, I'm from York.
Karen Oh, a Yorkie bar eh? A Yorkie bar.
Trish I could just eat some chocolate and all.
Karen You've just had your tea.

Trish And where's he from?
Andy Mars.
Trish Oh, you're a Mars Bar are you?
Tom Where are you from?
Trish Sheffield — we live in the same ... whatsit?
Karen Cul-de-sac.
Andy Right, right.
Trish What do you do then?
Andy He used to be a teacher.
Karen Oh, I hate teachers, all them holidays.
Tom Sorry about that.
Andy He's to blame for people like that. He's one of these who was against caning.
Tom I was against caning but I was pro-hanging. Are we er … ?

Barbie enters. She is completely soaked. And very angry

Barbie I don't believe it. I hope it's not going to be one of those weeks. But I've got a funny feeling it is. Gooor. Why me?
Trish Why did they do it?
Barbie I hate it; of all the shitty things in this job, this is the one thing I hate.
Andy Happens a lot then, does it?
Barbie Occupational hazard. They've just thrown a waiter in. It could be anybody next.
Trish Tom's looking after me …

Ray and Scott enter triumphantly

Scott moves upstage, takes a running jump and lands on Tom's back. He begins to chant. Everyone laughs, even Tom

Scott We are England, we are England, we are England.
Ray We are England, we are England.
Andy I think we're in the wrong hotel.
Barbie OK let's get down to Lennon's, shall we?
Scott Oh ay oh ay oh ay oh ay. (*He goes over to Trish*) Come on, you.
Trish Oh ay, look out.
Ray Oh ay oh ay oh ay oh ay oh ay.
Karen I told you your luck was in, didn't I?

Scott takes Trish off

Scott (*off*) In the pool in the pool.

Trish (*off*) Tom …
Scott (*off*) Just trust me.
Trish (*off*) I don't trust anybody.
Karen (*looking at Ray*) God, look at this one.
Ray You'll be all right with me.
Karen Come on then, Arnold. Let's see if Ringo's down at *Lennon's*.

Karen and Ray exit

Barbie (*moving towards the exit*) If you fancy a drink … ?

She exits

Tom and Andy relax

Tom Oh, yes — this is what they want.
Andy Are we going down?
Tom Are we hell.
Andy Why?
Tom You're joking, aren't you?
Andy We could drift down.
Tom What for?
Andy Check it out.
Tom Ooohhhh …
Andy Come on, what's … ?
Tom Come on — I mean — ohhhh.
Andy For a laugh.
Tom A laugh, are you serious? What's the point?
Andy We can just go for a drink.
Tom There's fifty million bars here, why don't we find another one?
Andy What's wrong? They won't bite.
Tom Don't bank on it, man, I mean them two, ooooh?
Andy Who's talking about them two?
Tom Who else is there, one's wet through and them two are sniffing. They're not my … you know?
Andy Don't judge a book by its cover.
Tom It's their territory, let's leave it. It'll be a bloody jungle down there …
Andy They're just bits of kids, we could handle them. Me and you.
Tom What are you talking about?
Andy We could.
Tom What are you saying?
Andy Well.
Tom We've only been here an hour and you're talking about aggro.

Andy No …
Tom Andy, the last time I had a fight I was eleven.
Andy Come on.
Tom You go if you want. Tell me all about it tomorrow. Just don't catch anything.
Andy Come on, hey, we're on holiday.
Tom What about the golf? I thought we had to be up early?
Andy I know, but just this once …
Tom It's a quarter to twelve already.
Andy It's still early.
Tom I've still got to phone Gail.
Andy Call her tomorrow.
Tom It's not fair.
Andy Let's just go for an hour. Just an hour. I mean, I'm wide awake anyway. We'll have a burger, have an hour and call that it.
Tom Hey, look, this is not what I expected.
Andy Yeeeah, come on …
Tom I dunno.
Andy Just one night, surely.
Tom No.
Andy Well, I'm ——
Tom That's fine ——
Andy There's only one key.
Tom I'll leave the door open.
Andy Come on ——
Tom No.
Andy For a crack?
Tom No.
Andy Oh, yeah.
Tom I'm sorry …
Andy Yeah.
Tom No. No. No.

Loud music

Black-out

SCENE 3

The hotel exterior. Day

The Lights come up very bright and the music fades

Background noise of holidaymakers can be heard. Andy is onstage braving the heat, still dressed, feeling and looking awful. He puts out his tongue, tastes his mouth, feels his head

Tom enters with a glass of orange juice

Andy Oh.
Tom Uh?
Andy Ah ooh.
Tom You.
Andy Eh?
Tom Honestly ...
Andy A good night …
Tom Time is it?
Andy Ten to eight …
Tom Oooo, yer has …
Andy I haven't drunk so much ——
Tom Never again, I mean that … That's it. I'm utterly disgusted with myself. I'm banning myself from drink, discos and dim women.
Andy (*breaking into a laugh*) I thought you weren't into discos.
Tom Don't. I've still got to ring Gail, she'll have a fit.
Andy I didn't know you could dance.
Tom I've been to Wigan Casino, old cock.
Andy Twenty years ago.
Tom My legs were going that fast my kneecaps were burning.
Andy You were sweating like an 'orse.
Tom I thought I was gunna pass out.
Andy I tell you something, you scored a hit last night.
Tom Get away.
Andy With mucky Trish.
Tom Don't.
Andy I think we're in.
Tom Bloody hell, give it a miss.
Andy Same again tonight, eh?
Tom No …
Andy Same again …
Tom I don't think ——

Andy You arranged to take 'em out.
Tom What?
Andy Yeah.
Tom Oh, shiiii …
Andy Paella, you said.
Tom Oh, shit.
Andy I think we are well and truly in, mate.
Tom No, I spent the whole of last night talking bollocks to a woman who washes hospital sheets. We are not in, no way.
Andy We are.
Tom They're not even our type.
Andy Variety is the spice ——
Tom Please ...
Andy Don't you like 'em?
Tom Yeah, but ——
Andy Well, then. If you hadn't've gone to university you'd've married somebody like Trish.
Tom Hey listen, Andy, really … ?
Andy Don't you think?
Tom You know what I'm like, I mean, come on.
Andy I never met women like that when I was young. All the girls I knew had ponies, and read *Little Women*. I didn't have a tongue in my mouth till I was sixteen — Sandy Jones, ooohhh.
Tom Don't, I feel sick as it is.
Andy Oh shit.

A moment

Tom Yeah.
Andy Why did we ever get married?
Tom Eh?
Andy Why?
Tom Well, I mean, how about love?
Andy Give me five good reasons.
Tom I can't think of five.
Andy Give me two then.
Tom I can't think of any at the moment.
Andy All those women out there and we got married.
Tom Why, you're happy enough, aren't you?
Andy Trouble with me is I'm never satisfied.
Tom No, well ——
Andy D'you want to know something, Tom, I think I'm an anarchist.
Tom No, you're not, you're an Executive in a Bread Firm.

Andy I feel like breaking things up, changing the *status quo*.

Pause.

It's too straightforward.
Tom What is?
Andy My life. Get up, go to work, earn money, come home, play with the kids, bottle of wine, nice meal. Go to bed, read, twelve o'clock—light off; go to sleep. Sex on bank holidays and birthdays. Visit family, go to supermarket, come home, cut lawn, watch cricket, bottle of wine, nice meal, go to bed. Pass "Go", collect two hundred pounds. Buy house. Sometimes I want to break it up.
Tom Sounds a bit like my life.
Andy Does it?
Tom But I don't have the bank holidays bit.

Pause

Andy Have you ever cheated on Gail?
Tom No. (A *beat*) Once, years back.
Andy Would you again?
Tom I feel like I already have.
Andy One night at a disco?
Tom What about you?
Andy No, no never.
Tom I don't believe you.
Andy Self-abuse has always been my style. It's safer.
Tom I wouldn't want to be growing up now.
Andy Ohh, a bloody mess. God knows what my young 'uns get up to.
Tom It's all in my head.
Andy Best place for it.
Tom Along with eight bottles of San Miguel.

They both laugh

Andy You ever paid for it?
Tom What?
Andy Have you ever paid for sex?
Tom What do you think I am?
Andy Just asking.
Tom I know we're sharing a room, Andy, but let's keep some things private.
Andy You're right, you're right.
Tom Have you?

Andy Not directly. The odd *à la carte* restaurant, this is before I met Lynne. Business dinners. I'd pick up the bill and then ohhhhhh … you know?
Tom So there was life before Lynne?
Andy I think so.
Tom That long ago?
Andy Another life.
Tom With me it was curries.
Andy Before Gail?
Tom Well before Gail. 1973 B.G.
Andy Ben Shermans?
Tom Clogs.
Andy Jesus, that's sad.
Tom I had some yellow loons and a fisherman's smock, I looked like a right twat. I was at university in Essex. The curry and coffee run we used to call it. You'd have a curry and then came that veiled euphemism: "Would you like to come back for a coffee?"
Andy "Would you like to see my etchings?"
Tom And then you'd sit until three o'clock in the morning, listening to "Hotel California" and talking about Piaget and deciding if she was going to stay and split the bed or go back to her digs. If you knew a caffeine addict you were OK.
Andy Does Gail know about all this?
Tom I've told her most things.
Andy Why?
Tom Because it's more straightforward.
Andy It isn't.
Tom No?
Andy So what about Karen and mucky Trish?
Tom Oh, leave it.
Andy They're good company.
Tom No, come on, let's hit the golf course …
Andy They'll've been dreaming about us, you know.
Tom You're joking, aren't you?
Andy Well, we can't disappoint them, can we?
Tom Play the game, Andy.
Andy I am.
Tom Play the game.
Andy I am.

Music

The Lights fade to Black-out

Scene 4

The patio area at the Hotel Rosamar. *Night*

The Lights come up and the music fades

Trish is sitting alone. She has obviously been waiting for some time

Karen enters. She is dressed up for the night. She looks attractive at first glance but then the image fades

Karen No — nothing.
Trish What?
Karen They're not in the bar.
Trish Might have gone.
Karen Obviously.

A beat

Trish What do you think?
Karen I think we've been stood up. Are you sure he said he'd take us out?
Trish I can't remember, to be honest.
Karen Oh, right. So we might have been sat here for two hours for nothing?
Trish Well, it's relaxing.
Karen I'm bleeding starving. What did they say?
Trish You were there as well.
Karen I couldn't see straight, we could've been talking to two donkeys for all I know.
Trish Oh, interesting.
Karen Hey, don't start.
Trish What?
Karen I know what you're thinking.
Trish What have I said now?
Karen You've got a dirty mind, you have.
Trish You have, you mean.
Karen Are they married?
Trish Dunno.
Karen They seem nice.
Trish Well, they're better than them two.
Karen We can leg it if you want — I mean I'm not … you know.
Trish They seem nice enough ——
Karen Don't trust 'em.
Trish Oh no …

Karen Nice sandals.
Trish Eh?
Karen My one had nice sandals.
Trish No, I didn't … it was too dark ——
Karen That's all I can remember ——
Trish Seemed nice though.
Karen Sandals.
Trish Did he have a beard?
Karen Why?
Trish He might have been a visitation.
Karen Beard and a donkey?

Andy appears upstage. He is wearing slightly prudish summer gear

Andy Here they are … hiya! (*He shouts off*) Tom! (*To the women*) We've been looking all over for you two.
Trish Have you?
Karen Well, you can't have looked far, I've been sat at the bar for an hour.
Andy No, we've been talking to a bloke about the bullfights. Trying to get tickets.
Trish Ohh no, I hate fights.

Tom enters, sheepishly. He is dressed rather casually and has a slightly ruddy face

Tom Hiya, all right?
Andy I was just saying about the ... er ...
Tom Yeah. Apparently. Friday, isn't it?
Trish Did you say you'd take us out, or not?
Tom Who?
Trish You.
Tom Yeah yeah. I didn't know whether or not you'd er … I mean, if you'd rather leave it?
Karen No … no … we're sat here.
Tom Sorry.
Karen You shouldn't stand people up, didn't your mother ever tell you that?
Tom No, that was one of the things she missed.
Karen Anyway, we forgive you, don't we, Trish?
Trish Thousands wouldn't.
Tom Oh right.
Andy Is everybody OK for a drink?
Trish We've just got one.
Karen Yeah, we've had four. Waiting.

Andy Tom … ?
Tom I thought we were doing without tonight?
Andy I'll leave it then. Shall I?
Trish How did you feel this morning?
Tom Rough.
Trish And me. My mouth — urghh!

Andy sits. It's awkward. Nobody knows what to say

Andy So what are you two doing tonight then?
Trish Well, I mean we were waiting …
Karen Depends.
Tom You're not going back down to *Lennon's*, are you?
Karen Might do.
Andy Great … fine. We are ——
Karen Might go and find two blokes to take us out.
Andy Good luck.
Karen We're waiting for an offer we can't refuse.
Trish You been golfing?
Tom I got an hole-in-one, yeah. Bang wooff.
Andy Beginner's luck.
Tom Hole in one with my first ball, but then — umphh. No.
Andy We went out on a pedalo.
Trish Oh, what is it?
Andy Well, you pedal it …
Trish Oh yeah?
Tom I think we stayed out too long, when we came back into land I was all over the place. I'm probably the only man to get seasick on a pedalo.
Trish (*finding this amusing*) I went on a ferry once.
Tom I'm still a bit … you know?
Trish Once, oh, never again, I hate boats.
Tom Me too.
Trish God, talk about sick, I threw my insides up I did, honest. Huuup. It was all coming up.
Karen Trish!
Trish I thought my stomach wall was coming up. Oh, I was bad.
Karen Yeah, you're making us bad now, aren't you?
Trish But I was sick though.
Tom He managed to push me in.
Trish Why?
Andy Accident. Just, you know, grabbed and then ——
Tom I can't swim. I was, you know, bloody water … umm.
Trish You should leave him.

Tom Yeah, leave me.
Andy Bloody accident. It was me or him … Boat went past and the waves went like whoooff.
Tom You should've seen me trying to get back on the pedalo. Talk about funny.
Trish I'll tell you what is funny ——
Karen Oh God, don't set her off.
Tom She was like this all last night.
Trish Listen, once I start ——
Karen Once she's off there's no stopping her.
Trish Did I tell you about our Tracey?
Karen Trish?
Trish It's true this.
Karen Not that about your Tracey, I can't stand it.
Andy Why, what is it?
Trish I tell everybody everything, me.
Tom Could be embarrassing.
Trish Our Tracey's at this party, right ——
Karen I've heard this a hundred times.
Trish — and she wants to use the loo ——
Andy Oh, I like those stories.
Trish — and she's dying to go, right, and there's somebody on the loo, so she runs into the garden and crouches down in the garden. Right. All done. Brilliant. No problem. Anyway. About an hour later she's dancing, right? And she can smell something.
Andy Oh no.
Trish Anyway, she has a feel about and you'll never guess what? She's got a turd stuck down the back of her cowboy boots.

They all find this funny

Tom You're funny.
Trish I'm not. Our Tracey is, you should hear it when she tells it.
Andy You bloody are.
Trish Am I?
Andy She's sexy and you're funny.
Trish Oh, thanks, you're funny but you're a dog.
Tom I thought funny was sexy?
Trish So did I.
Andy It can be.
Karen What are you then?
Tom Well, he's not funny.
Karen And he's not sexy.

Suddenly, Ray appears. He is drunk, and very red. He goes through the routine

Ray Oggy.
All Oh God … Oi.
Ray Oggy.
All Oi.
Ray Oggy Oggy Oggy.
All Oi Oi Oi.
Ray What you doing?
Karen Talking.
Ray Did you go to Wet 'n' Wild?
Trish Did we hell, she wanted to ——
Ray It was down on the beach.
Trish Look at him …
Tom That was me last night.
Ray Did you see me in *Lennon's*? I set fire to my hair.
Andy Oh, that was you, was it?
Ray Brilliant. Just put butane on it and whooof.
Andy What was the Wet 'n' Wild like?
Ray Wet and wild …
Andy Oh ay.
Ray You support Man U?
Andy Leeds.
Ray Leeds?
Andy Leeds.
Ray Leeds? Phooorr.
Andy That's right.
Ray Seen Scott?
Tom No.
Ray Hallo, Tom. Leeds? A good side when they're on form!

Ray mysteriously exits

Andy Oooh dear …
Karen Gooor eh? I've got one nearly that age. And he's a foul-mouthed gett. Isn't he? Our Grant?
Trish He's got a gob on him.
Tom You're both married then, are you?
Trish Was. She gave hers the push.
Karen Both young free and single, well, free and single.
Trish I was married at sixteen.
Andy Sixteen?

Trish I know, but I thought it was love.
Andy I still wanted to play for Leeds.
Trish He turned out to be about as much use as a chocolate fireguard. Then I married Dale when I was, what? Twenty, I think. We had ten years, that's not bad, is it?
Karen Ten years of hell.
Trish What about you?
Tom Thirteen years.
Trish Unlucky for some.
Tom Been married six, lived together.
Trish I wouldn't marry, not again.
Karen You got kids?
Tom Not yet.
Karen Not yet, what are you playing at?
Tom We like practising.
Trish What about you then?
Andy No.
Karen Kids?
Andy Not even married. Sadly.
Karen Nobody would have him.
Trish What about girlfriends?
Andy On and off. Nobody permanent.
Trish Ohh, that's a shame, innit?
Andy Luck of the draw, I'm afraid.

Tom is dumbfounded. Trish clocks this. Andy is embarrassed but has to play along with it

Trish Look at his face.
Tom What?
Trish Your face. I know what you are thinking.
Tom You don't.
Trish You're thinking "Shit" ——
Tom I am, you're right.
Trish — "Shit, I'm the only one here who's married." Am I right?
Tom No, you're a mile out.
Trish What are you thinking then?
Tom I'm just thinking, "Shit".
Karen He's crackers he is …
Tom I'm just thinking "Shit".
Trish Listen to him — a teacher.
Andy So are we having another drink or are we going down to *Lennon's*?
Tom I think I'll give it a miss.

Karen Ooohhhh, we're not good enough for you, is that it?
Trish Come on, Tom Tom Tom Tom Tom.

Ray returns with a bottle of San Miguel

Ray (*shouting*) Oggy.
All Oi.
Ray Oggy.
All Oi.
Ray Oggy Oggy Oggy.
All Oi Oi Oi.

Music

Black-out

Scene 5

Day. At the poolside

The Lights come up. The bright white of the stage should be blinding; the weather is baking hot. The music fades

Barbie is having a moment's relaxation, lying on a sun lounger with her eyes closed. She is working out the next trip. A bottle of sun block is nearby

Scott enters with a football

Scott Hallo.
Barbie Mmmm.
Scott You asleep?
Barbie Yeah …
Scott Hallo, hallo, hallo …
Barbie Don't.
Scott (*teasing*) Hallo.
Barbie Why don't you go and fall off a window ledge or something?
Scott I'll throw you off.

Silence. Scott stands and looks at Barbie. Then he looks around

Fit, ain't yer?
Barbie I'm asleep.
Scott You fit?

Barbie Mmmm.
Scott I am.
Barbie Are you?
Scott I should be …
Barbie Why?
Scott 'Cos I'm stacking crates every bleeding day, aren't I?
Barbie Are you?
Scott Never hardly see the sun … That's why I'm here, aren't I?
Barbie Is it?
Scott Get some sun.
Barbie Great. Let me just have five more minutes.
Scott Get some sun on my body …
Barbie Have you been abroad before?
Scott Yeah, I'm not thick.
Barbie No, right.
Scott I've been to Malta.
Barbie Yeah?
Scott Yeah!
Barbie Did you enjoy it?
Scott Naa, it's shit.
Barbie I've never been.
Scott It's shit.
Barbie I'll remember that next time we're picking resorts.

A pause

Scott It's shit. You hot?
Barbie Yeah.
Scott You sure … ?
Barbie Yeah.
Scott Arrrr.
Barbie What?
Scott Arrr, arrr, in the pool then ——
Barbie Oh no.
Scott Yeah ——
Barbie Don't.
Scott Thought you said you was hot?
Barbie Please, Scott, please don't, please.
Scott All right, but you owe me, right.
Barbie Right, yeah, right …

Scott sits. It is peaceful

Scott You down in *Lennon's* last night?
Barbie Not last night.
Scott Why do you always go to *Lennon's*?
Barbie (*sarcastic*) It's really great.
Scott Them two blokes were down there. Off their heads.
Barbie Really.
Scott They think they're it.
Barbie What were they doing?
Scott Dancing.
Barbie I thought you went to *Penelope's*?
Scott We did, got stood up and all, went down to *Lennon's* and they were there.
Barbie It's the luck of the draw.
Scott He's going in the pool that one.
Barbie Great. (*A beat*) Are you going to Aqualand?
Scott Yeah.
Barbie Give us a shout when the minibus comes, will you?
Scott You going?
Barbie Yeah.
Scott I'll give you a shout then.

Andy enters with some golf equipment

Saw you last night.
Andy Yeah?
Scott What were you supposed to be doing?
Andy It was supposed to be the Twist.
Scott You must be round the twist.

Scott exits

Barbie No golf?
Andy I went up there but … (*he reacts to the heat*) huuuuoo.
Barbie It's ninety.
Andy Do you play?
Barbie Actually I'm quite good.
Andy 'S scorching.
Barbie Go in the pool.
Andy I'm sure if I hang about long enough somebody'll throw me in. (*He surveys Barbie*) You all right there?
Barbie Yes, thanks.
Andy You got some oil on?
Barbie Yeah.

Andy Want any more?
Barbie No.
Andy What have you got on?
Barbie Total block.
Andy (*reading the label on the total block*) Oh right! (*He sits, across from Barbie*)
Barbie Play a lot of golf?
Andy Yeah.
Barbie My dad plays golf.
Andy Oh yeah?
Barbie It's an old man's sport, isn't it?
Andy No comment.
Barbie What's your handicap?
Andy Being here with Tom, I think.
Barbie What do you do?
Andy I'm a racing-car driver.
Barbie Oh, right.
Andy What did you do before you did this?
Barbie Brain surgeon.
Andy Oh, I see.

Tom enters. He is dressed in sports gear. He cannot take the heat

Tom How was it?
Andy Unbearable.
Tom It's too hot, there's no air.
Andy Have a dip.
Tom I haven't got the body for a dip, I've got more of a splash body.
Andy Have a splash then.
Tom Just phoned Gail again. Are we an hour in front or an hour behind?
Barbie In front.

Barbie exits

Tom That's three times and the answer machine isn't on.
Andy She'll be all right; if there was anything wrong they'd let us know, wouldn't they?
Tom They?
Andy Sorry.
Tom Who do you mean, they?
Andy Yeah, well ...
Tom Sorry?

They begin to whisper

Andy It just came out.
Tom Not much.
Andy Relax.
Tom Bloody hell.
Andy Just take it easy.
Tom I would but I don't know what you're going to come out with next.
Andy What about you on the dance floor? You're like a maniac.
Tom You're the bloody maniac. I thought you were going to eat her last night you were all over each other.
Andy Hey, come on. I'm just chilling out.
Tom Yeah, well, your chilling out is putting my nerves on edge. It's not so much that I mind you lying, it's that I've got to lie for you.

A beat

Last night that Karen was asking me all sorts about you.
Andy Like what?
Tom Like why didn't you ever get married? Did you never have anyone?
Andy And what did you say?
Tom What could I say?
Andy You didn't tell her the truth, did you?
Tom No.
Andy They probably didn't believe me anyway.
Tom I said that there was somebody once.
Andy Well, that's all right then.
Tom But she died.
Andy What?
Tom It just came out.
Andy She died?
Tom I just … you know …
Andy Anything else?
Tom No, that's it. Apart from the fact that you're a Barnardo's boy.
Andy You're joking?
Tom I was just saying anything.
Andy You bloody were, weren't you?
Tom I don't like all this, you know? I mean, what about Lynne?
Andy What about Gail?
Tom I'm not doing anything.
Andy Oh, right — what was all that Lam-bloody–bada stuff then last night?
Tom Hey, come on — I like her, but ——
Andy Listen, me and Lynne have always had an open marriage.

Tom Does she know that?
Andy She had an affair before we had our Verity. A bloke from the science department? They were at it all the time. I caught them in the garden shed once, and they weren't potting plants.
Tom You're not going for the full bizzo, are you?

Karen enters. She is wearing a bathing costume that is cut very tight and daring. She looks good but in no way perfect. The image is slightly broken by the presence of a cigarette in her mouth. She makes her way to a lounger

Karen Oooohh, ninety-four it is. Going to be like this all week according to Carlos at the bar.
Tom Juan.
Karen You what?
Tom His name's Juan.
Karen He looks like one and all. (*She enjoys the joke*)
Andy I call him Carlos. He still answers me.
Karen Aren't you going on a pedalo today, Tom?
Tom Not today.
Karen I thought you'd be out there scuba-diving again.
Tom Yeah, I swim like a stone.
Karen What about the golf?
Tom No … Beginner's luck I'm afraid.
Andy I had to stop him playing, there was no green left.
Tom Yeah, there was just turf everywhere.
Andy Too bloody dangerous, he is …
Tom Yes, I'm well under par.
Andy Ha ha.

Trish enters, wearing shades; she has a migraine and feels rough. She sits near the poolside

Trish Oh no, I feel bloody awful.
Tom Oh dear, here she is, Mother Teresa …
Trish (*to Tom*) It's your fault.
Tom What?
Trish You were trying to get me drunk.
Andy He didn't have to try very hard from what I saw.
Karen She drinks like a fish at home.
Trish When I've had a drink I'm completely out of control.
Tom We know that now.
Trish I was trying to keep up with you.
Tom You'll never do it. Drinking's my specialist subject.

Trish Oooh, help me, Tom Tom.
Tom Have another drink.
Trish Do you fancy one of them iced teas?
Tom Do you?
Trish We could share one.
Tom Do you want to sit in the shade?
Trish I want something.
Karen Go back to bed.
Tom Hey, steady.
Trish I think I'll make do with a tea.
Tom Shall I get us a tea and we'll sit in the shade?
Karen Yeah, get her in the shade …
Tom Shall we go and sit in the shade? This heat's no good for me, I'll come and read in the shade.
Trish Are you sure?
Tom Yeah, yeah — fine.
Trish Oh thanks, Tom.
Tom No problem.
Trish Isn't he sweet?
Tom Mind you, it must be sixty in the shade; we'll probably be the only people to go back with shadeburns!
Trish Isn't he lovely?
Tom I'm just doing the crossword, we can do it between us if you like. I'm stuck on a clue actually.
Trish Well, I'm no good.
Tom Here listen, "A postman's round, how many letters?"
Andy Oh no.
Tom "A bag full."
Trish A bag full of what?
Tom A bag full of bloody letters, you nit. It's a joke.
Trish I know that.
Tom What?
Trish I've heard it. It's that old it's got whiskers on.
Tom Come on, let's get some shade.

Trish and Tom head for the exit

Andy If you see Pablo ask him about them tickets for the bullfight.
Trish How hot is it in the shade?

Trish and Tom exit

Andy They make a right couple.

Karen He's got an admirer there.
Andy Yeah.
Karen Am I brown?
Andy Yeah … well, *going* brown.
Karen Am I hell! Goooor, it's hot, innit? Mind you, if it was pissing it down we'd be complaining, wouldn't we?
Andy We would.
Karen Never satisfied, are we?
Andy No, never.
Karen Never satisfied: as soon as we get what we want, we bleeding well want something else.
Andy Very true.
Karen Human nature.
Andy The grass is always greener …
Karen It is.
Andy I know.
Karen I couldn't wait to be eighteen, I'm thirty-seven in August and now I want to be sixteen again.
Andy Sweet sixteen …
Karen And know what I know now.

Silence

Is he all right?
Andy Eh?
Karen He seems a bit ——
Andy Oh, he's like that, can't enjoy himself.
Karen Oooohhh.
Andy I think he's missing his ——
Karen Old lady?
Andy Yeah.
Karen Oh dear.
Andy Yeah. It's — erm — well, you know ...
Karen Why'd he come, if he was going to miss her?
Andy For a little — you know ——
Karen Little break?
Andy They're a bit — you know?
Karen What, uneasy?
Andy Yeah. She's very ——
Karen Nervous?
Andy Intense.
Karen Intense. Ooooh, is she intense?
Andy Yeah.

Karen I'm not.
Andy No.
Karen Never have been.
Andy Intense?
Karen Nervous. No. Me? Straight in …
Andy And me.
Karen You're very different, aren't you? You two?
Andy Yeah. He's, erm …
Karen Different. Shy, you know, like insecure.
Andy He's very, you know, up here. (*He indicates his head*)
Karen Problems?
Andy Bright. He's very sharp.
Karen Funny, isn't he?
Andy He's the funny one, I'm the sexy one.
Karen He's nice, soft.
Andy He thinks too much. Worries. Emotional, you know. Up one minute and then ——
Karen (*disparagingly*) Ooooh down in the dumps?
Andy Depressed.
Karen Trish likes … (*She nods to the spot where Tom had been*)
Andy Oh.
Karen Depression? Talk to her. She's had a bad, erm …
Andy What about you?
Karen Listen, I can cope. I love 'em and leave 'em. But her and men, it's a bleeding nightmare, I tell you. I could write a book.
Andy Oh dear.

Karen applies sun tan oil to her body; it's quite sexy to watch. Andy watches

Karen Hit her.
Andy Oooohh.
Karen All sorts. Violent man. Bad. He just walked out.
Andy Awful.
Karen She always goes for the wrong sort. I mean, he's married, isn't he?
Andy Well … you know …
Karen When the cat's away?
Andy I wouldn't know …
Karen I know all about all that, make your toes curl up.
Andy Yeah?
Karen But you've not had it all easy, have you?
Andy Me?
Karen He told me.
Andy He never?

Karen I had a friend from Barnardo's.
Andy I don't like to talk about it.
Karen No. And your wife, I mean, sounds awful.
Andy It was.
Karen He said she choked.
Andy Eh?
Karen Choked.
Andy Yeah.
Karen On a fish bone?
Andy That's right.
Karen Weird.
Andy Yeah.
Karen Couldn't you do anything?
Andy Well, I patted her back. But I mean, what can you do when your number's up?
Karen He said it was violent.
Andy Awful, there she was choking — what could I do?
Karen Must have changed your life.
Andy Well, I can't eat fish any more.
Karen Oooh no.
Andy It cut me up.
Karen Listen, we're all scarred, darling. We've all got skeletons dangling in the cupboards. And those who say they haven't are bleeding liars.
Andy Funny thing, Karen, but sometimes it feels like it's just me who's hurting.

Karen needs help reaching her back with the suntan lotion

Karen You couldn't give us a hand, chuck, could you? Just on my shoulders.

Andy moves to Karen and takes some suntan lotion in his palm. He is nervous about it

Andy (*rubbing the lotion on Karen*) It's a long time since I've done this.
Karen Ohh, that's nice.
Andy Good.
Karen Yeah.
Andy You smell — erm …
Karen Oily?
Andy Yeah.
Karen Well, I am, aren't I? I'm covered in the stuff.
Andy That good?
Karen A bit firmer, darling … oh, that's good, yeah.

Andy Up here … (*He massages higher up her neck*)
Karen Oh my neck. You're good, aren't you?
Andy That OK?
Karen You could do it all day for me.
Andy Well, there's nothing else to do.
Karen It'd tire you out.
Andy No problem.
Karen Mmmmmm.
Andy Mmmmmm, feels good.
Karen You've got nice hands.
Andy Yeah?
Karen Cultured. My husband's hands were like great slabs. He couldn't control 'em. Do under my costume, that's where I burn.
Andy Oh right. Under? Right. (He *applies oil lower down her back*)
Karen You've got small hands, haven't you, for a man?
Andy Have I?
Karen I like small hands on a man.
Andy They're not that small, are they?
Karen They are compared to my husband, darling, he'd make two of you.
Andy Glad he's not here in that case …
Karen That's two of us.
Andy That it?
Karen That's ace. Ta.

Andy kisses Karen's neck

Mmmm.
Andy You smell … mmmm ...
Karen Oh dear. (A *big stretch*) Oooooh.
Andy Yeah.
Karen Oooohhh.
Andy Oooh dear …
Karen Hot innit?
Andy It is.

A beat

Yeah, it is … It's absolutely boiling.

He nibbles her neck. She drops the back of her head into his groin

Music

Black-out

ACT II

Scene 1

A balmy night, five days later

The Lights come up on the patio area

Tom sits alone onstage. He passes the time. Trish enters all dressed up for the night's barbecue

Trish Sorry.
Tom No problemo.
Trish What do you think to this … (*Her outfit*)
Tom Well?
Trish All right for a barbecue, isn't it?
Tom "Good is not the word."
Trish Eh?
Tom Noël Coward.
Trish You're full of 'em, aren't you?
Tom No, it looks good that. I'm staying with the more traditional boring man outfit.
Trish Oh, I like that outfit.
Tom You'd like it in our office then.
Trish I thought you might be dressed up like a matador.
Tom I did think about it but I couldn't find a three-cornered hat. And the trousers, I'm sorry!
Trish A bit too bright?
Tom And tight.
Trish Oh.
Tom Hey you.
Trish Steady.
Tom Exactly.
Trish Nudge nudge.
Tom You've got a dirty mind.
Trish I have.
Tom Did you enjoy it?
Trish A waste of money.
Tom It didn't cost us anything, Andy paid.
Trish Oh, I hate the sight of blood at the best of times.
Tom You what? You were screaming your head off.

Trish I was the one screaming for the bull.
Tom It's supposed to be the highest form of conflict. The bull's muscular power against man's initiative.
Trish Oh well, I dunno, but if you asked me the bull didn't stand a chance.
Tom I wouldn't do it, I'll tell you that much.
Trish They were just provoking it, no wonder it was bleeding mad.
Tom Hemingway described it as the "noblest" of all sports.
Trish You're off again. It's like being with a bloody library.
Tom Old habits, you see.
Trish I don't go on about hospital bed linen, do I?
Tom I wish you would, sounds interesting.
Trish No, I don't think so.
Tom Don't put yourself down all the time.
Trish Old habits, you see.
Tom *Touché*.
Trish You know what the worse thing was, don't you? When they cut its ear off. I mean they killed the poor thing, then cut its ear off. I wanted the bull to win. It should've ripped him apart, stuck its horns in him and ripped him open.
Tom You didn't like the matador then?
Trish (*enjoying the banter*) No, his trousers were too tight.
Tom I'm glad you warned me.
Trish Oh, don't set me off again. Once I'm into trousers I can't stop.
Tom Can't stop what?
Trish Talking about 'em.
Tom Oh right. What time is it?
Trish Not bored with me, are you?
Tom No no.
Trish Oh. I thought ——
Tom You're joking, aren't you?
Trish I know I can go on, I'm a bit bleeding dull at times.
Tom I wouldn't say dull.
Trish What would you say then?
Tom Well, erm, how about funny?
Trish You're worse than Andy. "Funny but a dog," he said. It's like this bloke on the plane, he was trying to get past us, so I says look out, and then he says, "Excuse me, ugly." I thought, "Oh well, thanks, baldy."
Tom You're not a dog.
Trish I'm not drop dead good-looking, am I?
Tom Would you want to be?
Trish No … too late now, anyway.
Tom You're thirty-one.
Trish Yeah, but I'm a lived-in thirty-one, aren't I?

Tom Well, I'm a lived-in thirty-eight. Gail's a lived-in thirty-four. Andy's a lived-in sixty.
Trish What's she like?
Tom Who?
Trish Your wife?
Tom God, I don't know. Where do you start? She's bright.
Trish (*encouraging*) Yeah well, that's a start and … ?
Tom She's very bright. She's kind. Moody, witty, attractive, sensible, loving, giving, homely, ambitious ——

Trish snores

— doubting, insecure …
Trish Who isn't?
Tom Bright.
Trish You've said bright.
Tom Have I? Trusting.
Trish I only asked a simple question.
Tom Cuddly toy, electric kettle, Whirlpool washer, microwave.
Trish She funny?
Tom Not hilarious, like you.
Trish What am I?
Tom Well, I don't really know you, do I?
Trish Do a list thing.
Tom I can't.
Trish Make it up.
Tom What was Dale like?
Trish Well, honestly, couldn't you sort that out for yourself? I mean, Dale, he wasn't a surgeon, that's for sure. Dale? I didn't notice at the time, then every time I said his name I burst out laughing. Dale? I looked it up in a dictionary once, it means an undivided field or a gulf. A great big gulf between what he said and what he did.
Tom How would you describe him?
Trish A dale, a male, a fail, a jail, a bail, and then in and out of jail again.
Tom You should be on the telly.
Trish Yeah, as an agony aunt.
Tom What was your sex life like?
Trish What is this?
Tom I'm a journalist, I get used to asking difficult questions.
Trish Tell me anything. Well, Doctor, it was rough and ready.
Tom Oh, rough, eh? Right.
Trish It wasn't all right, I didn't like it like that really. In fact, I didn't like it at all really. In fact, I think it's overrated. I'd rather have a good laugh.

I mean, you can have a good laugh anywhere, can't you? And you don't have to wear a condom. Mind you, it'd be funny if you did. Give a whole new meaning to Stand-Up Comedy. (*She sits*)

Tom (*moving close to Trish*) You.

Trish What?

Tom Goooooorr.

Trish What?

Tom You must know that I think you're …

Trish What?

Tom Very …

Trish You think I'm very ... oh well, that's nice. We've spent the last week together and you think I'm very …

Tom (*groaning*) Oh, words are shit, aren't they?

Trish Some are.

There is a pause

Tom I dunno.

Trish Confused, aren't you?

Tom I am.

Trish I am, but I don't think about it.

Tom Good idea. I'll try not to think about it.

Trish It works for me.

Tom Well, if it's good enough for you it's good enough for me.

A beat

I was just thinking that I really like you.

Trish I know that, Tom-tom.

Tom Is it that obvious?

Trish No.

Tom Well. I wondered if it would be all right if I kissed you.

Trish I think you'd better not.

Tom Right.

Trish I mean I've never been asked before.

Tom No?

Trish I think you'd better leave it.

Tom I've always been shit at kissing anyway.

Trish You're not that bad, are you?

Tom I'm too sloppy.

Trish Oh, one of them?

Tom Rubber lips, that's me.

Trish Let's have a see, just kiss my cheek.

Tom kisses Trish's cheek

Yeah, a bit sloppy.
Tom I did warn you. (*He sits beside Trish*)
Trish Isn't kissing weird?
Tom Making love is weirder.
Trish Is it?
Tom I think.
Trish Just touch my face.

Tom touches Trish's face gently, then begins to stroke it. She closes her eyes; his touch is obviously very soothing.

(*Softly*) It's nice that, it's nice. You're not very touchy, are you? You know, physical?
Tom Well. I dunno.
Trish I mean, we've been together for a week now and you've not touched me. Not even tried to.
Tom Sorry. Next time I'll be like an octopus.
Trish We haven't even kissed, have we?
Tom We have, just then.
Trish I think it's been romantic.

A beat

Tom So where have Andy and Karen been today?
Trish I wonder.
Tom Funny how Andy gave both tickets for the bullfight to me. I wonder why.
Trish She said they were going golfing.
Tom And if you believe that you'll believe anything.
Trish They haven't got around to the heavy stuff yet.
Tom How do you know?
Trish She tells me everything. Now, he *is* touchy.
Tom Andy — tell me about it.
Trish All over her.
Tom He's all over me half the time.
Trish Mr Touch he is.
Tom Not much.
Trish He needs a bloody strait-jacket.
Tom He'd probably get out of it, he's that slimy.
Trish Shall we have a drink while we're waiting?
Tom Well, it's a bit early for me.

Trish What, too early for a drink?

Tom Yeah, I can't drink until after nine, if I drink in the day I have to wear a balaclava. I can't drink in the daylight: anyway, look at this. (*He points to his stomach*) Too many love-handles.

Trish Middle-age spread.

Tom I have a fantasy that one day I'll be thin.

Trish I have this fantasy about going to bed with a man where nothing moves.

Tom Oh, very nice.

Trish You know, everything's solid.

Tom Can't help you there.

Trish Beautiful but shallow, that's me.

Tom I don't like taking my shirt off; I might frighten the children. I've got a runny body, you see. Like cheese. I've got a body like Brie. If I take my shirt off it runs all over the place. It's messy.

Trish The original Mr Blobby, blobby blobby.

They enjoy each other's fooling around

Tom (*meaning more than his words*) Oh, you ...

Trish Don't …

Tom In another life.

Trish Oh, don't, honest.

A beat

Tom In another life.

Trish Well — maybe we'll meet somewhere in the afterlife.

Tom I'd like that.

Trish So would I.

A beat

Tom Well, I must say I'm looking forward to tonight.

Trish So am I. It'll be brilliant.

Tom Three thousand raving maniacs at a barbecue in the mountains.

Trish I bet it's a riot.

Tom I bet it is. Three thousand spotty eighteen-year-olds swarming around tons of chicken wings is what I call a decent night out.

Trish You know what you are, don't you?

Tom I'm the funny one.

Trish You're a boring bastard that's what you are. I want to get up there and stuff myself stupid.

Andy and Karen enter. He is dripping in aftershave and is already slightly pissed. Karen is done up like a dog's dinner; she totters and smokes and is carrying a camera

Andy Are we ready then?
Tom Once more into the beach?
Andy (*to Trish*) God, you look good, kid. (*He kisses Trish*)
Trish He's full of shit, that one.
Karen And you're not wrong there.
Tom Phoor. How much bloody aftershave have you put on?
Trish A bottle-full: what is it, Blue Stratos?
Karen I can't smell it.
Andy It's Armani actually, but the bottle slipped.
Karen We've been up to Denia.
Tom What've you been doing up there then?
Karen Nothing. There's nothing to do.
Andy Did a bit of swimming.
Trish Very nice.
Karen The water's clear, isn't it clear, the water?
Andy A bit of the old skinny-dipping.
Trish Did she?
Karen What?
Andy She did. Straight off, everything came off: my eyes nearly came out of my head.
Karen He is such a liar.
Andy Yeah, had a little run in the car.
Karen He is such a one, he is.
Andy Didn't have a stitch on.
Trish I bet it's nice though.
Karen Oooohh, nothing there.
Andy Oh yeah, before I forget. *Pase oosteth, por favor, hay el telephono el recado.*
Tom What?
Andy There's a telephone message at reception.
Tom From Gail?
Andy Either her or the Queen.
Tom What's it say?
Andy What am I, psychic?
Tom Is it urgent?
Andy Dunno.
Tom Well, what did it say?
Andy Just to call. Don't get in such a panic.
Tom I'll just nip and see what it is. I'd better just nip ... It's probably nothing but ——

Tom exits

Trish (*to Karen*) You two look great.
Karen (*calling after Tom*) Don't be long, I want to get some photos.
Andy Look at him, off like a shot. That's marriage for you.
Trish Are we having some photos at the barbie?
Andy Don't take any photos of me, I'll break it.
Karen No, it'd be nice that, to keep.
Andy I never take a good picture. Never had a good one taken in my life. I always look backward.
Karen Maybe you are?
Andy I should have taken some of her today.
Karen Get away.
Andy I'm serious.
Karen Isn't he a pig?
Andy I'm not.
Karen Come on, let's have a photo.
Trish Shouldn't we wait for Tom?

Ray enters, smarter than we have seen before

Karen Hey sunbeam, take a picture, will you?
Ray What with?
Karen This camera, you thick git.
Trish Shouldn't we wait?
Karen No, come on, he'll have one after.
Ray Oh right, brilliant. Smile then. All say sex. Ha ha ha. Come on, get some spirit into it, you're like a set of crinklies.
Karen I'll gob him in a minute.

Andy is grabbed by Karen and Trish; they pose with their thumbs up for the camera. Ray takes a picture; the camera flashes

Ray Brilliant that, they could use that for next year's brochure.
Trish Why, don't they want anyone to come?
Ray What?
Andy All ready for tonight then?
Ray Yeah.
Andy Got your chat-up line ready? What is it? Oggy oggy oggy? It'll never catch on.
Ray That's not my chat-up line.
Andy Oh right.
Ray I haven't got one, to be honest.

Andy No?
Ray Have you?
Andy A hundred and one.
Ray Really?
Andy Yeah.
Ray Give us one then.
Andy Get your own.

A very attractive and smart-looking Scott enters with Barbie

Karen Oh, look at these.
Scott Well, sometimes you've got to make the effort 'aven't you? I'm sorry but I know I look like a god.
Trish Listen to him!
Scott I thank you. Join the queue, ladies. It's Barbie first and then if there's anything left I'll let you know.
Ray I'll have what's left.
Trish You been in the sun then?
Ray He has, I haven't, it's too hot. Burn my head.
Karen I thought you liked burning your head.
Ray Yeah, I did, but it's burnt, innit?
Andy Well then, Barbie, are you ready for the barbie?
Barbie You got some tickets then?
Andy Me know Pablo.
Barbie Sounds like you've been enjoying the Happy Hour.
Karen Tequila slammers. We've had three already.
Andy Oh yes, I think so. I'll show you what drinking is tonight, lads, just stand back and watch.
Ray Go on then, grandad.
Andy Oh, very nice.
Barbie Throw him in the pool, Andy.
Ray No way.
Andy No?
Ray He'd never catch me.
Andy No, I say it's time for somebody else to go in the pool.
Karen Just you dare, I've been in once today anyway.
Andy Trish.
Trish Oh no no.
Andy Yes. In the pool, Trish.
Trish Oh don't, I've washed my hair.
Andy I think so.
Karen No, leave her.
Trish Oh don't.

Andy In the pool.
Scott Yeah.
Ray In the pool, in the pool …

Andy runs to grab Trish and Ray helps him

Trish struggles, breaks away and runs off

Barbie stands to one side

The men follow Trish off. There is a massive cheer. Andy, Scott and Ray return

Karen Did you get her?
Andy No, she jumped in.
Barbie (*shouting*) Coward.
Scott Suicide mission.
Ray She jumped in the deep end. Just straight in the ten foot.
Andy We'll get her tomorrow. (*He shouts to Trish*) We'll get you tomorrow. Hey, let's chuck that German bloke in.
Scott We'll get him tomorrow.

Tom enters

Tom Can't get through. Bloody engaged. What was the message, Andy?
Andy I gave you the bloody message.
Tom Yeah, but … I mean, you know what Gail's like when she's probably on to your Lynne.
Karen Who's Lynne?
Andy My sister. Are we moving it?
Tom Where's Trish?
Scott She had to go in.
Tom Oh right, that's mature.
Andy It's just a laugh, mate.
Tom Who threw her in?
Scott She just jumped in.
Tom Oh yeah?
Karen She did, she's barmy.
Tom I don't think it's funny.
Andy She jumped in the bloody ten foot.
Tom Get off, man.
Scott I say we throw you in …
Tom Don't be stupid …

Scott You saying I'm stupid?
Tom Look, I'm not getting into this ——
Scott I'm not stupid.
Ray Smack him, Scott.
Andy Oh, very good — yeah.
Ray You should watch him, he's lethal.
Tom Look, forget it ——
Scott I'm not stupid, mate.
Tom No, sure, fine …
Scott OK?
Ray Smack him, you said you wanted to.
Tom I'm the stupid one, OK?
Ray (*to Tom*) He'll kill you, he will.
Scott D'you want to make something of it?
Andy Actually ——
Tom Andy, Andy, for God's sake … Look, forget I even said it — OK? I didn't mean anything by it …
Scott I'd throw you in but I don't want to mess my stuff up.
Tom That's a good job then, isn't it?
Karen Oh, come on, let's leave it …
Andy Yeah … yeah …
Barbie OK, come on, let's make some tracks. Here we go …
Scott Here we go, here we go …
Ray Lucky, very lucky.

Scott and Ray exit

Barbie exits separately

Karen (*shouting off to Trish*) Hang on, girl, I'll come and give you a hand. Look at her.

Karen exits to help Trish

Andy Look at that … (*He looks off after Karen*) Oh man …
Tom Is there any way of getting back from this ranch?
Andy Only by taxi, anyway you'll love it, it's a privilege to be there.
Tom Yeah, I can see that.
Andy Right, here we go. Here we go, here we go ...
Tom Please?
Andy Oh yes, man, makes you feel alive.
Tom Does it?
Andy This is better than bloody golf. We're in …

Tom Are we … ?
Andy Course we are.
Tom Do you think I should phone back?
Andy Oh, bloody leave it. Come on. We're laughing, mate!

Music; a large fiesta of sound, a massive carnival atmosphere

The Lights fade

Scene 2

The poolside. Morning

The Lights come up brightly. The music fades

Tom is splayed out on a lounger, asleep

Andy enters upstage. He is half-dressed, his shirt open and loose. He is absolutely tired out but strangely elated

Tom (*stirring*) Eh …
Andy Are you asleep?
Tom I was.
Andy Did I waken you?
Tom 'Time is it?
Andy Late.
Tom It's early, isn't it? Where've you been?
Andy What a night. (*He laughs*) Whooooo …
Tom What was it like?
Andy The Borgias. Why are you sleeping out here?
Tom There's only one bloody key.
Andy Sorry. What happened to you?
Tom I had to phone Gail, didn't I?
Andy Jesus.
Tom I just did.
Andy You left the biggest orgy on earth to phone your lass?
Tom I knew there was something, I just wanted to talk to her.
Andy And?
Tom My mum's had a funny do.
Andy Oh.
Tom It's not serious. Anyway. So I didn't feel like coming back up.
Andy No problem. But whoo. (*He sings*) "Oh what a night."
Tom What time did it finish?

Andy No idea. But I've never seen anything like it. At the end everybody was either naked, topless or pissed.
Tom Which one were you?
Andy All three.
Tom I bet.

Andy stops and looks at Tom

Andy Oh, man.
Tom Never again?
Andy Oh, man.
Tom What?
Andy You are going to freak.
Tom I'm too tired to freak.
Andy Oh, man.
Tom So where've you been?
Andy Oh dear.
Tom Don't tell me.
Andy I've done the naughty stuff.
Tom Oh no.
Andy I've done the bizzo.
Tom Oh, eh … no … eh … oh.
Andy The bizza was done.
Tom Who with?
Andy Who do you think?
Tom Sounds like it could've been more than one.
Andy Karen — oh yeah — I think so.
Tom Oh no.
Andy Oh yes.
Tom Where?
Andy Her bedroom.
Tom Oh no.
Andy Oh yes.
Tom Oh no.
Andy Oh, man.
Tom You stupid ——
Andy I was careful.
Tom Careful?
Andy Yeah.
Tom Careful is not doing it.
Andy It was OK …
Tom I don't want to know.
Andy She had a bag full …

Tom I do not want to know.
Andy I'd never seen so many.
Tom Bloody hell.
Andy I have seen the future, and she works in a chemist's shop. Superb. Honestly — I'm talking ohhh.
Tom Oh, give it a miss.
Andy I'm serious. Completely uninhibited. Just — urgh — and ... you know?
Tom I don't want to know.
Andy Where've I been, man?
Tom Hull, Andy. Hull.
Andy I mean Lynne's great but ——
Tom Why did you do it?
Andy Eh?
Tom Why?
Andy Ooohhh, man.
Tom Tell me.
Andy It was an accident.
Tom An accident.
Andy Yeah.
Tom An accident?
Andy It was.
Tom How do you do it by accident?
Andy It just was.
Tom No no, I'm sorry. An accident is three killed on the motorway, an accident is egg on your tie, an accident is not shagging a divorcée from bloody pharmaceuticals. You don't just fall into the missionary position.
Andy We did.
Tom I knew you'd have to do the full bizzo, I knew it. You disgust me.
Andy Why?
Tom I just don't believe you're that thick.
Andy What's up, are you jealous?
Tom I could kill you, I could.
Andy Why, because you couldn't get it together?
Tom Don't, Andy.
Andy It's true.
Tom Just don't, Andy.
Andy Why did you come back, you could've been in there?
Tom Wow, big deal.
Andy I'm pathetic, aren't I?
Tom Jesus.
Andy (*sadly*) I'm a slag, aren't I?
Tom I don't want to know anything about it.
Andy I feel great and you're ruining it.

Tom I don't want to know.
Andy I nearly peaked on the bus coming back. Oh, man, sex on legs.
Tom You peaked at the airport. I ought to get a golf club and batter your brains in.
Andy Why? What's it done to you, what's it done to hurt you?
Tom I'll tell you what it's done, what I can't stomach. You are in that room going away at it, and there's Trish the poor soul in the other bed trying to get some sleep while you're slobbering all over her mate. I mean, be fair, the lass has had a bad time sexually as it is without you rubbing it in.

A beat

Andy Trish wasn't there.
Tom Eh?
Andy No, she wasn't there.
Tom Well, where was she then?
Andy I don't know, but she wasn't there.
Tom Oh, right.
Andy In fact, I don't think she came back on the coach.
Tom Oh, right.
Andy I think she said she was going off with somebody.
Tom Oh, right.
Andy I think.
Tom Oh, right.
Andy No, she certainly was not there …
Tom Wonderful, wonderful. That's fine, that's great if she wants to do that then fine, lovely, that's lovely. Shit. I feel about thirteen years old.
Andy I do and it's brilliant …

A bedraggled Ray enters

Ray Wanna play shots in?
Tom No.
Ray We can play two on to one if you want?
Tom I don't want.
Ray Good night last night, eh?

Ray drifts off

Tom What are we going to tell Gail and Lynne?
Andy Nothing.
Tom So you want me to lie for you, again?
Andy Just keep it buttoned.

Tom What about your kids, man?
Andy It was just one night.
Tom AIDS is real, you know, Andy.
Andy Oh, shut it.
Tom I mean, it's here, mate, (*he holds his hand up to demonstrate*) it's this close to us, it's right up in our face.
Andy I'm not thick.
Tom No no, that's right. I mean Karen is such a nice quiet lass, isn't she? I mean, she wasn't out here for the fellas, was she? No, no, she was doing a research project into Don Quixote. I mean, she's probably only had one other sexual partner.

A beat

This week.
Andy Button it, pal, all right?
Tom Are you threatening me?
Andy I'm saying button it.
Tom Are you threatening me?
Andy Button it …
Tom Oh right, so now you're threatening me.

A beat

Andy You just have to forget it, it's not your business.
Tom Lynne is Gail's friend.
Andy So what's that to you? Who do you think you are, Francis of Assisi?
Tom I knew this was going to happen.
Andy Why.
Tom Because I saw what you did when we first arrived here.
Andy What?
Tom You put your wedding-ring in the security box.
Andy I always do that.
Tom I knew this was going to happen. You had it planned right from that first night, didn't you?
Andy No.
Tom You did. I saw you watching Trish and Karen by the bloody pool, from out the window. Bloody hell and this happens every time you come away, does it?
Andy Lynne doesn't understand me.
Tom There's no wonder, is there?
Andy She's like a bloody fridge with me, man, talk about frigid, it's like making love to a corpse.

Tom Phoooooww, Andy, Andy …
Andy It's not me … It's not me. Give us a break; I need a bit of action. Come on. I didn't plan it, no way.
Tom I don't believe you.
Andy It was just a case of opportunity knocks.
Tom All right, Hughie Green, give it a miss.
Andy And it knocked and I scored high on the clapometer.
Tom You're a sad bloke, Andy.
Andy Am I?
Tom You are.
Andy Funny, I thought it was you.

Silence

Funny, isn't it?
Tom No, it's anything but funny.
Andy It is, it's really funny. I was feeling really old at the beginning of the week, now I feel about sixteen again. Can you remember all the excitement you felt about going to the Christmas dance or to the youth club? When you knew nothing about women? When the most you could wish for was a tongue job off Sandy Jones? Cooorr, those were the days. Did you have those days? You were just a spotty-faced kid drinking Tizer and chewing gum, but you looked great in your cheesecloth shirt and you smelt of Brut, and all the women around you were wearing musk. And there you were stood by the boys' bogs waiting to catch a glance. Ooohhhh, fantastic, and you were desperate for Baz Shuttleworth the DJ to play "Coz I Luv You". Sixteen, Tom, sixteen, twenty-two distant years ago … That's how she made me feel, and the beat goes on.
Tom I wonder who she was with then?

A beat

Andy And the beat goes on.

Music

The Lights fade to Black-out

SCENE 3

The poolside. Day

The Lights come up brightly; it is obviously burning hot. The music fades

Trish and Karen are lounging by the pool, both wearing sunglasses. They are a little unhappy with each other. Karen behaves quite loudly and nonchalantly as if nothing has happened

Karen You sent any cards?
Trish Four.
Karen I haven't had time.
Trish No, no, that's right.
Karen Oy, what are you on about … ?
Trish Well, I mean, you and Andy … You know.
Karen Oh, come off it, Trish, you and Tom have been playing Romeo and Juliet all week.
Trish I don't know what I'm doing, half the time.
Karen Forget about it, it's yesterday. Enjoy the weather. Don't kill yourself.
Trish It was your idea to come.
Karen You said Spain.
Trish Centre Parcs.
Karen You never, you said Spain for the passion.
Trish I said Centre Parcs, we should've all gone to Centre Parcs, kids and all.
Karen Oh, leave it out.
Trish It's nice, and we wouldn't have put pressure on ourselves.
Karen Why, don't they let men into Centre Parcs?
Trish You know what I mean.
Karen If you don't want to get burnt stay out of the kitchen.
Trish I'm not blaming you.
Karen I mean, it was no great shakes. The lights certainly didn't go out for me, it wasn't the *1812* or whatever the hell it is. In fact, it was like 'em all, a feeble fumble.
Trish Makes you wonder why we bother.
Karen I reckon Andy's married.
Trish Yeah?
Karen Yeah.
Trish How do you reckon that then?
Karen Underpants.
Trish Yeah?
Karen Very bad underpants.

Trish It's always a sign, you should've seen Dale's.
Karen Yeah.
Trish What a liar then …
Karen And he kept his socks on …
Trish No — that wouldn't do for me. Kills it.
Karen Goooor.
Trish What?
Karen I was just thinking, how long … ?
Trish What?
Karen Since the last time?
Trish Who?
Karen Me.
Trish What about that bloke with the washers?
Karen Whirlpool man? No.
Trish You told me ——
Karen No.
Trish (*astonished*) Oh what, you liar.
Karen (*laughing*) Yeah, I know, I'm all gob I am.
Trish So what about you and that — that what's-his-face?
Karen Sam?
Trish Yeah.
Karen No, not really.
Trish You and Steve must have …
Karen That clumsy lump, he didn't come near me for years. And I mean years. Big useless dog he was.
Trish I thought you were always ——
Karen Steve?
Trish Well, I mean — I thought.
Karen Hardly ever — I mean, at the beginning, but after our Grant, no, not really. Just sort of drifted apart. He never touched me really.
Trish I thought … you know?
Karen Four years. Four years since. Goooor, what a wait eh? He never touched me for all that time.
Trish I don't believe you.
Karen Four years, I swear. Four years I've waited and when it happened it was over in a blink.

Pause

Bloody awful he was.
Trish Yeah.
Karen Awful … No style, know what I mean? No control. And to top it all he leaves his socks on.

Trish Is this what we came for?
Karen We came for the sun, didn't we?
Trish Yeah.
Karen Well we got that, didn't we?
Trish Yeah, we got that all right.

Andy enters. He looks and feels ill

Trish He's here, the oldest swinger in town.

Andy sits. The atmosphere is very awkward between them

Andy Hallo.
Karen Hi.
Andy All right?
Karen Yeah yeah.
Andy Good.
Karen Yeah.
Andy Feel all right?
Karen Ready to go jogging, I am.
Andy Great.
Karen Yeah.
Andy Where did you get to?
Trish That's for me to know and you to … (*She touches her nose*)
Andy Very disappointed, my mate. Tears, everything.
Karen Where is he?
Trish He's probably on the phone.
Andy (*to Karen*) Listen, you don't fancy a bit of a walk, do you? I fancy walking this head off.
Karen Oh, go on then, twist my arm.
Andy I'll treat you to a coffee.
Karen Oh, that's big of him.
Andy Come on then.

Andy helps Karen from the lounger. It is awkward; we see how difficult they are with each other physically. As they stand:

Tom enters with a newspaper He is bright and cheerful, as if he is completely untouched by recent events

Karen moves to Andy, making a gesture to him with her little finger

Tom Morning.

Karen Oh, the party pooper!
Tom Sorry — but you know what it's like.
Andy We're having a saunter, are you in for it?
Tom Erm … No … no, I'll just …
Andy Right. Have fun..

Karen and Andy exit

Trish and Tom watch them depart. Tom sits and reads his paper. There is silence

Tom Mmm.
Trish Yeah.
Tom (*stretching*) Oh...
Trish Tired?
Tom You must be.
Trish I'm all right.
Tom Warm again.
Trish Mmmmm.
Tom They reckon it'll be in the nineties again today.
Trish That's hot then.
Tom Yeah.
Trish Home tomorrow.
Tom That's right.
Trish Raining in England.
Tom As usual.
Trish Three inches in London.
Tom Yeah?
Trish Typical.
Tom Tomorrow night.
Trish Back to reality.
Tom That's about it.
Trish Well, have a good life.
Tom Yeah.
Trish Good.
Tom And you?
Trish I'll try.

Pause

Tom I'm sorry about last night.
Trish There's nothing to be sorry about, is there?
Tom It wasn't really my scene …

Trish You had to call your wife, didn't you?
Tom Yeah, my mum. Tired herself out. She has these funny dos with her heart. Hospital job, I'm afraid. She's all right. Gail just needed to talk to me. Anyway I suppose it was safer.
Trish What?
Tom If I'd've stayed anything might've happened.
Trish No.
Tom We'd've only made a fool of ourselves ——
Trish I can do that any time.
Tom Felt guilty this morning.
Trish Well, I had a brilliant time.
Tom Good.
Trish Met a bloke.
Tom (*with difficulty*) Good.
Trish Yeah.
Tom Was he nice?
Trish Yeah.
Tom Anyone I — ermm … ?

A beat

Trish No.
Tom No — no, right …
Trish Yeah, he's a nice bloke. Mind you, that's probably all I'm good for, isn't it? You know, going out, having too much to drink and then picking somebody up.
Tom Well, if that's what you want.
Trish It isn't what I want.
Tom Well, you could've fooled me.
Trish You're such a snob.
Tom Me?
Trish You.
Tom I'm not.
Trish You are.
Tom Well, what are you then?
Trish You've got a bleeding nerve, haven't you?
Tom What?
Trish You come all the chat.
Tom I meant it.
Trish "In another life?"
Tom Yeah.
Trish They're only words to you, aren't they? Only words. They don't actually mean anything.

Tom Actually they did.
Trish No, they never. And do you want to know what the joke is? I actually had thoughts, I actually let myself have thoughts about you. I let myself imagine things. That I might see you when we got back. I actually let myself believe that when we got home we'd start seeing each other and before you knew it we were a couple. I must be bleeding crackers.
Tom I feel like that, I mean, you're great.
Trish Pull the other one …
Tom Trish, you're wonderful, you are.
Trish Thanks for that.
Tom Look, I'm sorry.
Trish Thanks, for being sorry.
Tom You could have come back with me if you'd've wanted.
Trish How could I? I didn't know what to do.
Tom No?
Trish No.
Tom Well, it didn't take you long to find somebody else, did it? Mind you, like you said it's probably all you're good for.
Trish That's right. A quick lay is all I'm good for!
Tom You said it.
Trish At least I've got the bottle to do it.
Tom Oh wow, yeah, "Hold the front page".
Trish I'm not frightened of it like you.
Tom That's right, it scares me shitless.
Trish Do you know, I bet it does and all?

Silence

Tom Hey, look — this is very childish.
Trish Will you go, please?
Tom Hey, Trish, sorry …
Trish Go, please …

Silence

I'm waiting for somebody.
Tom Oh, I see.

Scott enters, brash and confident

Scott All right then, Drum man?
Tom Eh?
Scott Tom-tom. All right, Trish?

Trish Yeah.
Scott Couldn't take the pace, eh?
Tom That's right.
Scott Tosser.
Tom Yeah. I had to finish a book.
Scott Old age, mate …
Tom Something.
Scott (*to Trish*) Good night, wasn't it?
Trish Yeah.
Scott We're going down for some breakfast, wanna come?
Trish What's wrong with the hotel?
Scott No, it's that continental shit. We want a proper English job.
Tom That's right, none of this foreign muck, eh?
Scott That's it, set you up for the day that will. A bit of sausage and black pudding, you'll be laughing.
Trish Where are you going?
Scott Geordie's on the back street.
Trish I'll come after.
Scott You'd better.
Trish I will. Yeah, I will.
Scott Going back tomorrow, aren't you?
Tom That's right.
Scott Oh shit, and I didn't get to throw you in the pool.
Tom Pity.
Scott Yeah. Yeah, it is.

Scott exits

Silence

Tom Right then.
Trish Right. (*She makes to go*)
Tom Going for breakfast?
Trish No … no.
Tom I thought you and him ——?
Trish Oh, give me a break, will you? Me and him, what d'you think I am? I'm not that hard up, you know?
Tom I thought ——
Trish Yeah, well, it was just a snog. You've got a dirty mind, ain't yer?
Tom Oh, Trish … I'm sorry, I thought, God knows what. I mean, hey, Trish …
Trish It was just another suicide mission that's all.
Tom I think you're ——

Trish Yeah, you think I'm "very".

A moment

Anyway, I'm going for a walk along the front. I'm serious, you know: if you're ever down our way, look me up, we'll have a laugh, and that's all. I mean that — just a laugh.

Tom Yeah, not even half a bizzo.

Trish pecks Tom on the cheek

Trish Anyway, there you go, one-all.
Tom I'll come with you, shall I?
Trish What for, Tom-tom, it's pointless?
Tom I'll just come for a laugh, shall I, just for a laugh?

Trish exits slowly. Tom follows her

Music

The Lights gently fade to Black-out

Scene 4

The poolside. The following night

The Lights come up. The music fades

Ray is sitting by himself. He appears to be down. Barbie enters

Barbie Are you coming down to *Lennon's*?
Ray Dunno.
Barbie Are you OK?
Ray No.
Barbie Why?
Ray My head's still killing me …
Barbie That'll teach you.
Ray It usually doesn't burn so much.
Barbie I thought you were enjoying it?
Ray I hate it at *Lennon's.*
Barbie Why?
Ray Because you always take us there. Are you getting a backhander or something?

Barbie (*defensively*) No.
Ray Oh yeah?
Barbie Just the odd drink, that's all.
Ray Get off; you're making a right packet, I'll bet.
Barbie Who me, would I do anything like that?
Ray Anyway.
Barbie What?
Ray I can't stand it. I can't sleep at night because it's too hot. The noise in the disco is sending me around the bend. The women ignore me, and I haven't worn any of the clothes I've brought. I just can't handle it.
Barbie Well, it is fairly hectic. Didn't you expect it to be like this?
Ray Yeah, this is my fifth Club holiday. I always come to Benidorm. And I never meet anyone.
Barbie Well, maybe next time?
Ray No.
Barbie Why?
Ray This is the worst holiday I've ever had.
Barbie How do you think I feel when you say that?
Ray Yeah, but you're getting paid.
Barbie You've had a good time, haven't you?
Ray I'm looking for something though …
Barbie Join the club.
Ray I wish I was going back.
Barbie Tom and Andy'll be getting on their way now, why don't you go and swap them? I think Andy wants to stop.
Ray I would but it's a Manchester flight.
Barbie Anyway, I thought you were big mates with Trish and Karen?
Ray Naaa.
Barbie They'll be down at *Lennon's* later.
Ray Yeah, with two other crinklies probably.
Barbie I thought women loved your mate?

A beat

Ray How long have you been out here?
Barbie A long time.
Ray Don't you ever meet anybody?
Barbie Is that an offer?
Ray No.
Barbie Oh, I'm disappointed.
Ray I mean, yeah.
Barbie Ah, too late …
Ray Yeah yeah, it is an offer.

Barbie I asked but obviously you're not interested ——
Ray It was an offer, honest …
Barbie Holiday romances never last, do they?
Ray Dunno, do I, I've never had one.

Scott enters, slightly drunk

Scott Right, come on …
Ray What?
Scott Down to *Lennon's.*
Ray Orhh.
Scott Yeah.
Ray No.
Scott Yeah.
Ray Naaa.
Scott Why not?
Ray It's boring.
Scott Listen, I'm in …
Ray You are, but what about me?
Barbie Well, get down there, Ray, shake your body …
Scott I'm in.
Ray Who with …
Scott Never you mind.
Ray That Trish? Naaa.
Scott (*affirmative*) Hallo? Hallo? I think so.
Ray I don't.
Scott You what?
Ray I don't think you're in.
Scott Come on, man, we'll string 'em along for a laugh.
Ray They're too old ——
Scott No way, they've got experience.
Ray What's the point?
Scott What do you mean?
Ray Oh, forget it ——
Scott What do you mean?
Ray Forget it.
Scott Barbie, are you coming?

A beat

Barbie Yeah, I might as well.
Scott See.
Ray Yeah.

Scott See, this is what you do.
Ray Is it?
Scott We're on holiday, you twat!
Ray I know.
Scott So let's go and have a good time!
Ray Naaa.
Scott Look, we've got two weeks a year.
Ray I know.
Scott Now I'm gunna enjoy it if it fucking kills me. I'm gunna do what I want. Right. Right. Right, Barbie?
Barbie Right.
Scott If I want to throw somebody in the pool, I will. If I want a snog, I'll get one. If I want to get blasted off my face, that's OK. OK?
Ray Yeah, I know, but …
Scott No buts. No buts. No excuses, no wimpy buts. I'm tired of buts, I get buts at home. I tell you what you should do, you should take up golf that'd suit you.
Ray I might meet more people.
Scott And then you'd be like them two swarmy twats. I tell you what why don't you wear sandals and all, and have wine and cheese evenings?
Ray They're not interested in us, though?
Scott Ray, Raymondo, we work, we work, right? We lift crates all day every day, and we get paid shit and then what happens? Then we die. And when we're dead we can't say: "Oooh, I wish I was back in Benidorm. Oooh, I just fancy going out and having fish patty and chips. Ohh, I think I'll go down to *Lennon's* and try and pull some fluff." Because you will be dead, and you will be thinking, "Shit! Shit, I didn't even try with Karen and Trish."
Ray I know.
Scott So get your arse up off of that, and let's get down to *Lennon's*, and do something. We are doers, Golf man. Did you know that? We are doers. We're not thinkers, we're not frightened of the world, we're action men.
Ray Awwwwwrr!
Scott Come on … come on … no more talk, up and off. Let's get down there and pull some tash. Hey, Barbie, come here ——
Barbie No.
Scott Yeah. (*He is obviously keen to give Barbie a hug*) Giz a kiss …
Barbie Maybe later. I'll see you down there. It should be a good night: I mean, who knows, Ray, anything could happen?

Barbie exits. They both watch her go

Scott (*ignited once more*) Yes … ! Yes, hear that, hear that, you spineless golfing gett.

Ray I'm in, I think I'm in …
Scott We are in …
Ray I'M IN!
Scott "Maybe later", that's all you need. A maybe. A maybe is as good as a yes.
Ray Is it?
Scott A maybe is what makes you live, Raymondo. A maybe is a sign.
Ray Is it?
Scott Course it is.
Ray Is it?
Scott It's all we've got. We may be in with Karen and Trish, and we may be in with Barbie. (*He almost begins to sing*) I love it. I love this country … oh, I love this sunny Spain. Oh, viva España!
Ray Oh shit …
Scott Sing Ray.
Ray (*singing the "Stingray" tune*) Sing, Ray. Sing, Ray.
Scott Here we go, here we go, here we go.

Loud music

Black-out

SCENE 5

The dining-room of Tom and Gail's house. A few days later

The Lights come up. The music fades

Tom and Gail, Andy and Lynne are enjoying a dinner party. Candles burn, everyone is laughing

Tom pours himself another large glass of wine

Lynne So how's your mum?
Tom What a fiasco, honestly.
Andy What happened?
Tom The last report has it that: my dad was on the loo, his usual place, and he was constipated, hadn't been for a fortnight; anyway apparently he was pushing too hard and passed out, collapsed against the toilet door, my mother freaked, heard the noise, it started her heart racing, she fainted, and when our Susan passed, moments later, she found the two of them unconscious with three ton of shit in the loo.
Gail Tom?

Tom And now they're not talking for another forty years. (*To Andy*) They've sworn an oath of silence.
Andy (*to Gail*) So what's new, gorgeous?
Gail Wined and dined by half the Humanities department, but apart from that it's more of the same.
Lynne We went to Alton Towers — have you been?
Andy Typical, once my back's turned she whizzes off with my credit card.
Tom Sweet revenge.
Lynne I'll take Andy and show him a good time.
Tom Yeah, he likes a good time.
Gail So, go on then?
Tom What?
Gail What was it like?
Andy The golf, you mean?
Lynne They didn't meet a soul according to Andy: is that right, Tom?
Tom (*uneasily*) That's right.
Lynne I can't believe that. He usually goes on and on about some golfing farts he's thrashed.
Tom Yeah, he's a right little Ballesteros.
Gail I bet they were out every night.
Andy Not every night.
Lynne They wouldn't tell us anyway.
Andy We would.
Tom We did meet two women actually.
Andy Did we?
Tom Yeah.
Andy I can't remember.
Tom Can't you?
Andy Can you?
Tom Very clearly.
Andy It's all a blur ——!
Tom There was Barbie.
Andy That's one.
Tom And Trish.
Andy That's right, those two … yeah …
Tom And Karen.
Gail That's three.
Andy Yeah, we were just talking to them one night.
Tom Was it just the one?
Andy Ibiza women we call 'em, don't we? (*To Lynne*) Denim and inlaid leopard skin.
Tom They were nice actually.
Andy It's all a haze to me.

Tom Don't worry, mate, I've got it all stored, up here. I've got a memory like an elephant. Almost total recall, I've got.
Andy I can't remember much of it at all. (*He yawns*)
Lynne Tired?
Andy We should go soon.
Tom You must remember Karen?
Andy Eh?
Tom Karen.
Andy Well, I do.
Tom I thought you might.
Lynne I think we'd better think about going.
Tom Yeah, you must remember Karen?
Andy Well, yeah.
Tom Dark woman.
Andy Yeah, yeah …
Tom A bit of an alchemist...
Andy It's coming to me now, yeah …
Tom Worked in rubber?
Andy That's right …
Tom Quite a shy woman …
Andy Trish's mate.
Tom Yeah, liked skinny-dipping.
Andy Did she?
Lynne I think we should go. Or we might hear something we don't want to.
Andy Yeah, and I might hear how much you've spent on my credit card.
Lynne Come on, then. Let's hit the road.
Tom Don't you want to stay 'n' hear about Karen and Trish?
Andy He's pulling your leg, he is.
Lynne We haven't seen each other for ten days, you know?
Tom No no, that's right. I'd better let you both go. Eh, get back, tuck into the fridge.
Andy Into the fridge, yeah, very good.

Andy and Lynne get ready to leave. Andy kisses Gail

Take care … see you soon.
Tom We can talk about it another time if you want.
Andy That'd be good.
Tom We could probably get some photos sent from 'em.
Andy God, I'm knackered.
Tom Too much bed eh …
Andy Excellent.
Tom Yeah yeah.

Andy Cheers, mate.

Kisses all around. Andy shakes Tom's hand and hugs him

I love this man, we should go away more often.
Tom Yeah great, can't wait.
Andy I love this man.

Lynne exits

Gail I'll call you.
Andy I love that man. That man is a god!

Andy exits

Tom and Gail sit in silence

Gail He gets worse.
Tom Yeah.
Gail What was he like … ?
Tom Ooooo?
Gail So what's all this about Karen and Trish?
Tom Karen was one for the trophy wall. He must be at it every time he goes out there.
Gail Don't tell me, I don't want to know.
Tom I've got to tell somebody.
Gail I'm not interested.
Tom Yeah, well.
Gail So what about Trish?
Tom Trish.
Gail Yes.
Tom Trish is — er …
Gail Oh, come on.
Tom Trish was funny.
Gail Oh, right …
Tom I really liked Trish, actually …
Gail Oh?
Tom And like I said to her, in another life … ?
Gail You said what … ?
Tom In another life …

Silence

Gail Oh right.

Tom Yeah.
Gail And what does that mean?
Tom She's great, she made me feel sad ——
Gail Oh, I see.
Tom She made me think.
Gail About another life, presumably?
Tom About you, about kids, about a lot of things.
Gail I hope you didn't talk to her about me.
Tom Why?
Gail What happened?
Tom Nothing.
Gail I don't believe you.
Tom Nothing happened.
Gail You've let me down once, Tom, and I don't believe you!
Tom It could have but it didn't. I fought it.
Gail Oh, wow, what do you want, a Blue Peter Badge?
Tom I felt comfortable with her, that's all.
Gail You fancied her, you mean?
Tom I did, yeah.
Gail I thought so …
Tom But more than that …
Gail She made you feel sad …
Tom Don't take the piss.
Gail So you had feelings for her?
Tom Well … Yeah. Sort of.
Gail Great. Great, you had feelings for her because she was funny. What was she, a clown?
Tom Hang on ——
Gail And I suppose I've stopped being funny, is that what you're getting at?
Tom Not at all …
Gail I'll tell you what, I'll wear some flippers and a snorkel. Will that make you feel sad?
Tom Hey hey ——
Gail Are you in love with her?
Tom It's not like that.
Gail Andy sleeps with somebody, which is bad enough, but you? You have to go the whole hog. You're not concerned with mere physical attraction oh no, that's not enough for you, is it? You have to fall in love with her, and run off and live in Barnsley or somewhere.
Tom Sheffield actually.
Gail Oh, you know all about her then?
Tom You know what I'm like, I'm pathetic, I mean emotionally pathetic. I'm soft, Gail, reasonable, understanding, educated and soft.
Gail But it happens every time you get to know another woman.

Tom But I feel sorry for her. I mean, what has she got? I don't know? I feel sorry for her because she hasn't got anything and she's lost and she's having to live her life all by herself.
Gail Oh, stop it, Tom, I'm crying …

Silence

Tom But you're not hearing me.
Gail Aren't I?
Tom Am I with the right woman, Gail? Do you think after all this time, am I with the right woman?
Gail Oh what?
Tom Yeah!
Gail Well, go then, go and find your Lady in Red.
Tom Am I though?
Gail Only you know that.
Tom I dunno …
Gail Is anybody?
Tom Exactly.
Gail Is Andy?
Tom A resounding no. Lynne isn't with the right man.
Gail Don't you think I ask the same question?
Tom Are we all fickle?
Gail The whole world is! Look at the bloody politicians! They're so fickle: as soon as somebody winks at them they stand there with their trousers down.
Tom (*confused*) I don't know.
Gail Do you want to see her again?
Tom Give up …
Gail Do you?
Tom No — I don't think so.
Gail You don't think so …
Tom No.
Gail Be honest.
Tom I'm trying to be.

A beat

Gail I knew when I saw you that you were off me.
Tom I'm not off you, I'm just sad.

A beat

Gail You can't be with everybody.

A beat

Tom I know — I know.
Gail You're thirty-eight, Tom, and you've just had your first holiday romance.
Tom I know and it's killing me.
Gail Just look at your mum and dad, never strayed. Never even contemplated it.
Tom Yeah, but you don't want to end up like them, do you?
Gail It could be worse.
Tom Will we ever speak "Grunt" … ?
Gail We do.
Tom Ah? (*He gives a very long and sad sigh*)
Gail Yeahhh.
Tom Forty years …
Gail Forty years.

Silence

Tom Will that be us … ?
Gail I hope so.

A beat

Gail picks up some things from the table and moves to exit

Tom Bloody hell, it's obscene.
Gail I know.

Gail exits

Tom goes to pour himself more wine. The bottle is empty

Music

The Lights fade to Black-out

FURNITURE AND PROPERTY LIST

ACT I

Scene 1

On stage: Dining table. *On it*: remains of dinner party with wine glasses and coffee cups
Four dining chairs

Scene 2

Strike: Everything from Scene 1

Set: Lobby Area
Chairs
Barbie's belongings, including a bag with a computerized chart in it

Patio Area
Chairs

Poolside
Sun loungers

Off stage: Large case (**Ray**)
Colourful holdall (**Scott**)
Luggage (**Trish** and **Karen**)
Bottle of beer (**Scott**)
Bottle of beer (**Ray**)
Bottle of beer (**Scott**)

Scene 3

Off stage: Glass of orange juice (**Tom**)
Bottle of *San Miguel* (**Ray**)

Scene 4

Set: Poolside
On sun lounger: bottle of sun block

Off stage: Golf equipment (**Andy**)
Cigarette, sun tan lotion (**Karen**)

ACT II

Scene 1

Off stage: Cigarette, camera (**Karen**)

Scene 2

No additional properties

Scene 3

Off stage: Newspaper (**Tom**)

Scene 4

No additional properties

Scene 5

On stage: Dining table. *On it*: remains of dinner party with wine glasses, coffee cups and candles
Four dining chairs

LIGHTING PLOT

Practical fittings required: nil
Composite set: a dining room, various interior and exterior parts of an hotel with exterior backing

ACT I

ACT 1, Scene 1

To open: General interior lighting on dining-room set

Cue 1 They all laugh. Music (Page 5)
Black-out

ACT I, Scene 2

To open: General interior lighting on lobby area of hotel with night effect on exterior backing

Cue 2 **Tom**: "No. No. No." (Page 19)
Black-out

ACT I, Scene 3

To open: General exterior lighting on hotel exterior and exterior backing — very bright

Cue 3 **Andy**: "I am." (Page 23)
Black-out

ACT I, Scene 4

To open: General exterior lighting on patio with night effect on exterior backing

Cue 4 **All**: "Oi Oi Oi." (Page 30)
Black-out

ACT I, Scene 5

To open: General exterior lighting on poolside and exterior backing — very bright

Cue 5 **Karen** drops her head into **Andy**'s groin. Music (Page 40)
Black-out

ACT II, Scene 1

To open: General exterior lighting on patio with night effect on exterior backing

Cue 6 **Andy**: "We're laughing, mate!" Music (Page 52)
Black-out

ACT II, Scene 2

To open: General exterior lighting on poolside and exterior backing — very bright

Cue 7 **Andy**: "And the beat goes on." Music (Page 57)
Black-out

ACT II, Scene 3

To open: General exterior lighting on poolside area and exterior backing — very bright, hot effect

Cue 8 **Tom** follows **Trish** (Page 65)
Gentle fade to Black-out

ACT II, Scene 4

To open: General exterior lighting on poolside — night effect on exterior backing

Cue 9 **Scott**: " ... here we go." (Page 69)
Black-out

ACT II, Scene 5

To open: General interior lighting on dining-room set

Cue 10 Music (Page 75)
Fade to black-out

EFFECTS PLOT

ACT I

Cue 1 They all laugh (Page 5)
Music; fade as SCENE 2 *begins*

Cue 2 **Scott** and **Ray** throw **Barbie** in the pool (Page 16)
Splash

Cue 3 **Tom**: "No. No. No." (Page 19)
Loud music; fade as SCENE 3 *begins and bring up background noise of holidaymakers (heard throughout* SCENE 3)

Cue 4 **Andy**: "I am." (Page 23)
Music. Cut holidaymakers' noise. Fade music as SCENE 4 *begins*

Cue 5 **All**: "Oi Oi Oi." (Page 30)
Music; fade as SCENE 5 *begins*

Cue 6 **Karen** drops her head into **Andy**'s groin (Page 40)
Music; fade when ready

ACT II

Cue 7 The men follow **Trish** off (Page 50)
Splash

Cue 8 **Andy**: "We're laughing, mate!" (Page 52)
Music; fade as SCENE 2 *begins*

Cue 9 **Andy**: "And the beat goes on." (Page 57)
Music; fade as SCENE 3 *begins*

Cue 10 **Trish** and **Tom** exit (Page 65)
Music; fade as SCENE 4 *begins*

Cue 11 **Scott**: " ... here we go." (Page 69)
Loud music. Fade as SCENE 5 *begins*

Cue 12 **Tom** discovers the bottle is empty (Page 75)
Music